COLORWORK CREATIONS

KNIT WOODLAND INSPIRED HATS, MITTENS AND GLOVES

SUSAN ANDERSON-FREED

KRAUSE PUBLICATIO
CINCINNATI, OHI

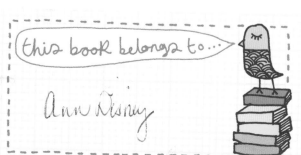
this book belongs to...
Ann Disny

Colorwork Creations

KNIT WOODLAND INSPIRED HATS, MITTENS AND GLOVES

SUSAN ANDERSON-FREED

Colorwork Creations. Copyright © 2010 by Susan Anderson-Freed. Manufactured in the USA. All rights reserved. No part of this book may be reproduced in any form or by any electronic or mechanical means including information storage and retrieval systems without permission in writing from the publisher, except by a reviewer who may quote brief passages in a review. Published by Krause Publications, a division of F+W Media, Inc., 4700 East Galbraith Road, Cincinnati, Ohio, 45236. (800) 289-0963. First Edition.

www.fwmedia.com

14   13   12   11   10   5   4   3   2

Distributed in Canada by Fraser Direct
100 Armstrong Avenue
Georgetown, ON, Canada L7G 5S4
Tel: (905) 877-4411

Distributed in the U.K. and Europe by David & Charles
Brunel House, Newton Abbot, Devon, TQ12 4PU, England
Tel: (+44) 1626 323200, Fax: (+44) 1626 323319
E-mail: postmaster@davidandcharles.co.uk

Distributed in Australia by Capricorn Link
P.O. Box 704, S. Windsor NSW, 2756 Australia
Tel: (02) 4577-3555

Library of Congress Cataloging in Publication Data
Anderson-Freed, Susan.
  Colorwork creations: knit woodland-inspired hats, mittens, and gloves
/ Susan Anderson-Freed. -- 1st ed.
    p. cm.
  Includes index.
  ISBN-13: 978-1-4402-1242-0 (pbk. : alk. paper)
  1. Knitting--Patterns. 2. Hats. 3. Gloves. I. Title.
  TT825.A557 2010
  746.43'2041--dc22

                    2010004742

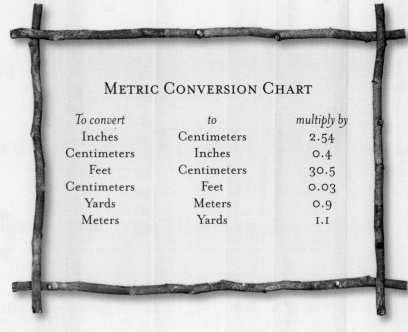

METRIC CONVERSION CHART

To convert	to	multiply by
Inches	Centimeters	2.54
Centimeters	Inches	0.4
Feet	Centimeters	30.5
Centimeters	Feet	0.03
Yards	Meters	0.9
Meters	Yards	1.1

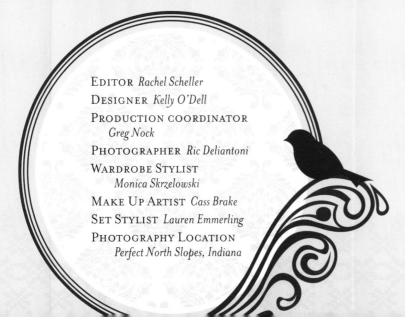

EDITOR *Rachel Scheller*

DESIGNER *Kelly O'Dell*

PRODUCTION COORDINATOR
Greg Nock

PHOTOGRAPHER *Ric Deliantoni*

WARDROBE STYLIST
Monica Skrzelowski

MAKE UP ARTIST *Cass Brake*

SET STYLIST *Lauren Emmerling*

PHOTOGRAPHY LOCATION
Perfect North Slopes, Indiana

DEDICATION

To the doctors, nurses and staff of Mid-Illinois Hematology & Oncology Associates, especially Dr. Pramern Sriratana, and to all those whose lives have been touched by cancer.

ACKNOWLEDGMENTS

Many individuals helped make this book a reality, and I would like to thank them for their support and encouragement. Thank you to Matthew Hesson-McInnis for first introducing me to knitting gloves from the fingers to the cuffs. Thanks to Deborah Barone for putting me in contact with Jennifer Claydon, an editor at F+W Media. Deborah also test-knit tams and mittens.

Thanks to Jennifer Claydon, who helped me through the initial book conceptualization stages. Thanks to my editor, Rachel Scheller, for guiding me through the production phases. Thank you to book designer Kelly O'Dell and to Ric Deliantoni, the photographer.

I'd also like to thank my husband, John, who tolerated the many bins of yarn filling the family room, and my daughter, Jenny, for test-knitting the tams and hats and gleefully pointing out pattern mistakes.

Finally, I'd like to thank the doctors, nurses, staff and patients of Mid-Illinois Hematology and Oncology Associates. I knit many of the items displayed in this book during chemotherapy and I received many words of encouragement during my weekly chemotherapy sessions. Finally, I would like to thank the volunteers and staff at the Community Cancer Center of Bloomington-Normal.

ABOUT THE AUTHOR

Susan Anderson-Freed learned to knit at the age of nine from her grandmother and has since passed along the craft to her daughter, Jenny. She retired as a Professor of Computer Science at Illinois Wesleyan University in July 2010 after more than thirty years of teaching. Susan lives with her husband, John, two cats and a Golden Retriever. She enjoys cooking, spinning, dyeing, weaving and, of course, knitting in her spare time.

TABLE OF CONTENTS

INTRODUCTION

When I was nine, my grandmother from the Upper Peninsula of Michigan came to our home in Green Bay for a weeklong visit. She brought along a set of double-pointed needles, a how-to booklet on knitting and a booklet of mitten patterns. During her visit, Grandma Enoch taught me how to knit. I fell in love with the craft immediately and made several pairs of mittens, the only thing I knew how to make at the time.

The only part I hated about knitting mittens was the thumbs. I wrestled with knitting those few stitches with the weight of the mitten body hanging down, threatening to pull my mitten stitches off their needles. The mausoleum of thumbless mittens in my basement is a testimony to my dislike of knitting the thumbs.

My attitude changed when my friend Matthew Hesson-McInnis gave my daughter, Jenny, a do-it-yourself high school graduation present. Matthew had created a pattern for men's gloves that began at the fingers and ended at the cuff. He wanted a similar pattern for women's gloves, and the beautiful silk and cashmere yarn he included with the instructions for the men's gloves was the only enticement I needed.

As I worked through Matthew's directions, changing the pattern to fit a woman's hands, I thought of the beautiful Fair Isle gloves and mittens I had seen in pattern books. Could I make these gloves and mittens from the fingers or crown to the cuff? Over the next ten years, I designed gloves and mittens constructed in this fashion. Matthew's original design, with its rounded fingers, elaborate gusset increases and decreases and little finger added after the initial fingers, did not lend itself well to Fair Isle knitting. Slowly, I developed patterns

and techniques that worked with a variety of knitting traditions, including Fair Isle, knotwork and Sanquhar.

When I embarked on my glove-making adventure, I recalled the lovely Sanquhar patterns that originated in the town of the same name in Dumfriesshire, England. I loved the little boxes of pattern and initially created my versions of the four traditional Sanquhar designs: Duke, Roses, Rose and Trellis, and Drum and Cornet. As a Professor of Computer Science, I couldn't resist the urge to place new designs in those little boxes—the number of possibilities was infinite. I added trees, stars and designs adapted from Anatolian sock patterns and Peruvian weaving patterns. As a cancer survivor since 1992 with an ongoing reoccurrence since 2004, I also designed the small bows so often used to signify cancer survival.

Once I constructed the gloves, I turned to adapting the designs to mittens. The patterns lent themselves well to mitten designs, especially when knit from the mitten crown down to the cuff. Salt-and-pepper rounds are used on the crown, and the Sanquhar patterns finish the mitten body. My friends and family encouraged my creativity by asking "Could you . . . " questions: "Could you make me gloves with fingers that end before the first knuckle?" or "Could you make me those flip-top mittens with a full thumb and a mitten hood?" My usual response was, "Maybe," and then I tried to accommodate their requests. The creation of fingerless gloves and flip-top mittens followed.

To give the pieces a woodland theme, I added beasts and birds to the backs of the gloves and mittens. I created these designs using a wide variety of sources. The reindeer combined Scandinavian knitting patterns and a lace pattern from the sixteenth century. The griffin was adapted from a pair of seventh century BC Scythian bronze statues featured in The Metropolitan Museum of Art bulletin. The butterfly began with a drawing of a tiger moth found in a field guide. However, the biggest influence on my designs was my father's bird carvings. The bird designs are based on these carvings as a way to honor my father's memory.

While I was designing gloves and mittens, I returned to my twenty-year fascination with tams. While most contemporary tams use a seven-point crown, traditional designs feature tams with a wide variety of points, although six-, eight- and ten-point crowns seem to predominate. Over the course of a year, I developed tam designs with crowns that had points ranging from five through eighteen. A few of my favorite designs are featured in the book.

The inspiration for the ski hats came from *A Shetland Knitter's Notebook* by Mary Smith and Chris Bunyan. Snuggled between the pages of text was a picture of Shetland hats featuring tam-like crowns. This was exactly the hat I wanted to design. I worked on designing bird and beast hats to match the mittens and gloves while choosing crown designs that would work with the bird or beast and border design of the hat.

My daughter's trip to Peru furnished the inspiration for the chullos, and a recent trip to Iceland further illustrated the popularity of earflap hats in a cold clime. These hats are a favorite among my nieces, and they keep my ears toasty on dog-walking excursions.

I think you'll discover that knitting gloves or mittens from finger or crown to cuff is far more pleasurable than cuff to finger or crown. A ski hat or chullo in a matching bird or beast design is a perfect companion to your pair of mittens, gloves or flip-tops. So enjoy!

FAIR ISLE KNITTING

I fell in love with Fair Isle knitting in the early 1990s. Imagine all of the gorgeous designs you can produce by using only two colors in any given round. Since knitting is in the round, the right side of the piece is always in front of the knitter. This results in fewer pattern mistakes and much greater knitting speeds.

BASIC TECHNIQUE

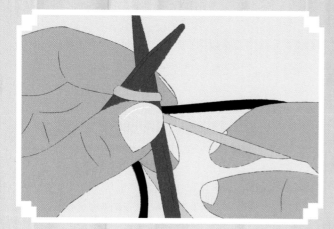

YARN PLACEMENT
I generally prefer to hold my yarns on either side of my middle finger as shown.

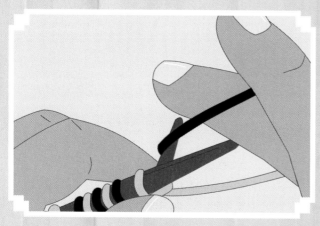

KNITTING WITH THE MAIN COLOR
To knit with the main color (MC) yarn, use the outside edge of your middle finger to lift the yarn into place.

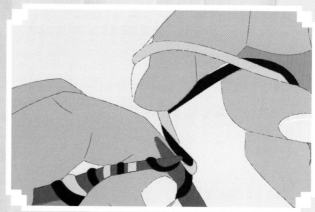

KNITTING WITH THE CONTRASTING COLOR
To knit with the contrasting color (CC) yarn, use the inside of your middle finger to lift the yarn into place.

READING CHARTS

Because knitting is in the round, you will read all charts from right to left. Since I don't like to count the stitches knit in each color, if a bird or beast pattern contains more than four consecutive stitches in the same color, I indicate that in the chart. In the following simple chart, the diamonds in Rounds 3 and 5 contain five consecutive red stitches. Rounds 1 through 7 each contain at least one set of five consecutive white stitches. Be careful to watch for consecutive stitches wrapping from the end to the beginning of the next pattern repeat.

CHART READING

YARN CARRIES

When a pattern indicates that more than three or four stitches are knit in a single color, always carry the yarn along the back of the work. To do this, simply flip the yarn not being knit over the working yarn. I also carry the yarns when I change colors. To do this, break off the old yarns and switch to the new yarns. Knit the pattern in the new colors. On the next round, tie the old and new yarns into a knot. As you knit each stitch, flip the yarn tails over the working yarn. Do this for ten to twelve stitches. Wait a few rounds before clipping the loose ends. Not only does this technique secure the loose ends, but it saves you time later.

TANGLED YARN

Inevitably, the yarns will sometimes tangle. To untangle them, simply place one strand of yarn in each hand. Let your knitting hang down. Your garment will start to spin, with each revolution removing one twist. It's quite fun to watch.

MATERIALS AND TOOLS

NEEDLES

The pattern directions for the gloves and mittens suggest one set each of 6" (15cm) and 8" (20cm) double-pointed needles in the size required for the indicated gauge.

I also prefer 10" (25cm) or 12" (30cm) double-pointed needles for the hats, tams and chullos instead of circular needles because they cause less wear and tear on my thumbs.

If you choose to knit your projects with alpaca yarn, I highly recommend bamboo needles because the yarn is less likely to slip off the needles.

As a final note, the needle sizes are based on my gauge. I knit very loosely. In contrast, my daughter knits much more tightly. When she test-knit several tams, she increased the needle size significantly. Always check your gauge before beginning a project to ensure the correct fit and to save time.

YARNS

I've knit the patterns in this book using a wide variety of yarns. Although I suggest specific yarns for each garment, most fingering-weight yarns work well. There are several fingering-weight yarns that I am still eager to try.

ROW COUNTER

This gadget comes in handy when working the corrugated knitting or salt-and-pepper rounds.

STITCH MARKERS

Since it's far easier to correct a mistake if it's discovered early, I use stitch markers to separate the pattern repeats for the tams, hats and chullos. After completing each repeat, I check to make sure that the repeat ends on the correct stitch.

SAFETY PINS

I use large quilting safety pins to hold the stitches on the fingers and thumbs when making gloves and mittens.

TASSEL MAKER

Each chullo requires three tassels. I've employed some creative tools for making tassels in the past, including a stack of index cards. I now use an inexpensive tassel maker produced by Susan Bates.

TAM FRAME OR PLATE

The tams require blocking over a tam frame or a plate. Since tam frames are hard to come by, a 9" (23cm) plastic dinner plate works fairly well. You can usually pick these up at a discount store.

CHAPTER ONE
HATS

In 2007, my niece requested a hat with a brim for Christmas. I suggested that she consider a tam. After a twenty-year hiatus from tam making, I was eager to try my hand at designing tams with varying points on the crowns. This began a yearlong adventure and the creation of more than seventy different designs. My daughter saw the simple, but colorful, tubes emerging from my needles and asked if she could try her hand at tam knitting. She was hooked after the first, eventually knitting more than twenty tams.

Both my daughter and I noticed that the recipients of our tams believed that these designs were difficult to knit. Nothing could be further from the truth. Tam knitting requires only two colors in any given round, and the crowns incorporate a simple double decrease. The only trick to tam making is beginning the crown from the center stitch of the wheel design.

The ski hats combine the Sanquhar and bird or beast designs with the crown designs used in the tams. As is true of the tams, the hats use only two colors in any given round. The crowns also use the same double decreases found in the tam patterns and require the same care in ensuring that the crown begins with the center stitch of the design. My daughter also took great delight in making several of these hats and found the knitting to be fairly easy.

Chullo knitting begins with earflaps that are knit back and forth. Since the design is only visible on the knit rows, care must be taken while working the purl rows. A purled 3-Needle join attaches each earflap to the chullo body on the hem round. Because the earflaps are identical, it makes no difference which earflap is attached first. The chullos use the same border and bird or beast patterns as the ski hats. They feature a crown design above the upper border to give them added height, and they end with a traditional triangular crown knit in a solid color. A classic chullo contains tassels attached to a knitted or braided rope dangling from each earflap and the crown. The i-cord tassels used in my designs are easy to knit and attach; however, if you prefer a more European earflap hat, simply leave out the i-cord and tassels. In central Illinois, where the wind blows cold in the winter, we tie the earflap i-cords together to keep the earflaps snugly against our ears.

Basic Hat Patterns

SKI HATS

The ski hat pattern begins with a selvage deep enough to cover the ears, thus providing a double layer of protection from the cold. The body begins with the border, followed by a bird or beast design and a second repetition of the border. Each hat ends with a wheel-shaped crown. The crown designs are interchangeable if you follow the instructions for increasing or decreasing the stitches prior to beginning the crown.

SIZE

Women's medium

NEEDLES

One set of 10" (25cm) US 2 (2.75mm) double-pointed needles or a 24" (60cm) circular needle

One set of 8" (20cm) US 2 (2.75mm) double-pointed needles (optional)

If necessary, change needle size to obtain correct gauge.

GAUGE

36 sts and 36 rows = 4" (10cm) in St st

SKI HAT

Using MC, cast on 145 sts. Join to knit in the rnd.

Rnds 1–16: Knit.

Rnd 17 (inc rnd): Knit while increasing 15 sts evenly—160 sts.

Rnd 18: Knit.

Hem Rnd: Purl.

Knit 3 rnds in MC.

LOWER BORDER

Foll the border chart for the desired ski hat.

BIRD OR BEAST CHART

Foll the bird or beast chart for the desired hat using a variegated yarn and natural/white.

UPPER BORDER

Foll the border chart as directed for the lower border.

CROWN

Foll the instructions and patt design for the bird or beast hat crown. It may be helpful to switch to the 8" (20cm) dpns as the number of sts decreases. Each crown contains a triangular grid coupled with written instructions for the decreases.

After the last rnd, draw the yarn through the remaining sts.

Turn the hat inside out. Fold the hem at the Hem Rnd and tack in place on the inside of the hat.

Weave in all ends and block.

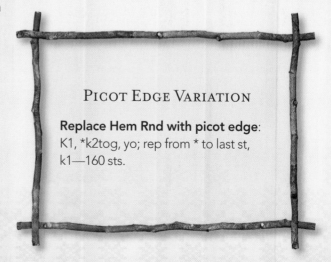

PICOT EDGE VARIATION

Replace Hem Rnd with picot edge: K1, *k2tog, yo; rep from * to last st, k1—160 sts.

CHULLOS

Chullo knitting begins with the earflaps, which are knit back and forth. The flaps have a garter stitch border that will curl in slightly after knitting; however, this can be remedied with blocking. The earflap charts are interchangeable, so you may use any earflap pattern with any of the border and bird or beast designs. Simply substitute the colors to match your chosen design. After each earflap is completed, attach an i-cord rope and a tassel.

The body of the chullo begins with a selvage for the hem. The earflaps are attached at the hem border by purling together a stitch from the earflap with a stitch from the chullo body. Each chullo contains a border, a bird or beast design, a repetition of the border and a crown design. Each of these elements is interchangeable among the chullos. The chullo ends with crown shaping that reduces the top to a point. An i-cord rope and tassel are attached to the top.

SIZE

Women's medium

NEEDLES

One set of 10" (25cm) US 2 (2.75mm) double-pointed needles or a 24" (60cm) circular needle

One set of 8" (20cm) US 2 (2.75mm) double-pointed needles

If necessary, change needle size to obtain correct gauge.

GAUGE

36 sts and 36 rows = 4" (10cm) in St st

CHULLO

EARFLAPS

Using MC and 8" (20cm) dpns, cast on 3 sts, leaving a 3 yd (2.7m) tail for the i-cord.

Row 1: Knit.

Row 2 (inc rnd): K1, m1, k1, m1, k1—5 sts.

Row 3 (inc rnd): K1, m1, k3, m1, k1—7 sts.

Row 4 (inc rnd): K1, m1, k5, m1, k1—9 sts.

Rows 5–41: Cont following the earflap patt for your chullo.

AT THE SAME TIME:

Work increases on the RS as foll: K3, m1, foll patt to last 3 sts, m1, k3.

Work increases on the WS as foll: K3, m1p, foll patt to last 3 sts, m1p, k3.

Row 42: Dec 3 sts evenly across the row—34 sts. Break off yarn, leaving an 8" (20cm) tail. Place sts on a holder or spare needle.

Using MC and yarn tail, pick up and knit 4 sts from the cast-on edge. Work 5"–6" (13cm–15cm) of i-cord (approx 28 rows). Bind off. Cut yarn, leaving a 10" (25cm) tail for securing the tassel.

Make the second earflap to match.

CHULLO BODY

Using MC, cast on 145 sts.

Rnds 1–6: Knit.

Rnd 7 (inc rnd): Knit while increasing 15 sts evenly across rnd—160 sts.

Rnd 8: Knit.

Hem Rnd: P15. Place the sts of the first earflap on a spare needle. Purl tog 1 st from the earflap and 1 st from the chullo body until all earflap sts are attached to the body. P62. Attach the second earflap using the same technique as the first earflap, p15—160 sts.

Knit 1 rnd in MC.

COLORWORK

Foll the border chart for the desired chullo.

Foll the bird or beast chart for the desired chullo using variegated yarn and natural/white.

Foll the border chart for the desired chullo.

Foll the chullo crown chart for the desired chullo.

Knit 1 rnd in MC, then cont with crown shaping.

CROWN SHAPING

Use MC. It may be helpful to switch to the 8" (20cm) dpns as the number of sts decreases.

Rnd 1: *K14, skp; rep from * around.

Rnd 2: *K2tog, k13; rep from * around.

Rnd 3: *K12, skp; rep from * around.

Rnd 4: *K2tog, k11; rep from * around.

Rnd 5: *K10, skp; rep from * around.

Rnd 6: *K2tog, k9; rep from * around.

Rnd 7: *K8, skp; rep from * around.

Rnd 8: *K2tog, k7; rep from * around.

Rnd 9: *K6, skp; rep from * around.

Rnd 10: *K2tog, k5; rep from * around.

Rnd 11: *K4, skp; rep from * around.

Rnd 12: *K2tog, k3; rep from * around.

Rnd 13: *K2, skp; rep from * around.

Rnd 14: *K2tog, k1; rep from * around.

Rnd 15: *Skp; rep from * around.

Rnd 16: *K2tog, k3; rep from * around.

Rnd 17: *K2tog; rep from * around—4 sts.

Work 28 rows of i-cord in MC. Bind off. Cut yarn, leaving a 10" (25cm) tail for attaching the tassel.

Make 3 tassels. Each tassel should be 4" (10cm) in length. Attach one to the i-cord at the end of each earflap. Attach one to the i-cord at the crown.

Turn chullo inside out. Fold the hem at the Hem Rnd and tack into place.

Weave in all ends and block.

TAMS

As a child, I was fascinated with kaleidoscopes, simple tubes that, upon twisting the top, produced a myriad of beautiful designs. Tams remind me of kaleidoscopes. When knitting the simple tube that forms the tam, I never quite know what the final product will be until I stretch it over a blocking plate. Changing the colors of a tam completely changes the appearance.

My daughter test-knit many of the tams I designed; however, her preferred color schemes were markedly different from mine. Experiment with the colors, and you will be surprised with the finished results.

ANATOMY OF A TAM

All tams begin with corrugated ribbing. Although this type of ribbing lacks the elasticity of k2, p2 ribbing, its vivid color changes produce a beautiful finished look. The technique used to produce corrugated ribbing is simple: knit two stitches in one color and purl two stitches in a second color.

Upon completion of the ribbing, knit two repeats of the tam brim chart. One repeat forms the lower brim, which you'll see when the tam wearer faces you. The second repeat forms the upper or top brim, which you'll see when the tam wearer has her back to you. The upper brim is followed by the tam crown design.

FINISHING YOUR TAM

To block your tam into a wearable circular shape, stretch it over a plate or tam frame. Begin by soaking the tam in a wool wash such as Eucalan. Remove most of the moisture from the tam by wrapping it in a towel or sending it through the spin cycle on your washer. Stretch the tam over a 9" (23cm) plate or a tam frame, and let it dry.

SIZE

Women's medium

NEEDLES

One set of 10" (25cm) US 2 (2.75mm) double-pointed needles or a 24" (60cm) circular needle

One set of 8" (20cm) US 2 (2.75mm) double-pointed needles (optional)

If necessary, change needle size to obtain correct gauge.

GAUGE

36 sts and 36 rows = 4" (10cm) in St st

BUTTERFLY SKI HAT

YARN

1 skein each of Knit Picks Palette (100% wool, 1.75oz/50g, 231yd/210m) in Huckleberry Heather (MC), Blush, Lipstick and Garnet Heather

1 skein Knit Picks Imagination Hand Painted Sock (wool/alpaca/nylon blend, 1.75oz/50g, 219yd/199m) in Damsel (variegated)

1 skein Knit Picks Bare Merino Wool, Silk Sock (wool/silk blend, 3.5oz/100g, 440yd/400m) in Natural (CC)

CROWN SHAPING FOR BUTTERFLY SKI HAT

Before beginning crown, knit 1 rnd in CC—160 sts. Knit 1 rnd in CC while decreasing 6 sts evenly across rnd—154 sts.

All decreases except Rnds 4, 7, 10 and 26: Sl 2, k1, p2sso.

Dec for Rnds 4, 7 and 10: Sl 1, k2tog, psso.

Rnd 26 dec: K2tog.

BUTTERFLY BODY (USE VARIEGATED YARN FOR BUTTERFLY)

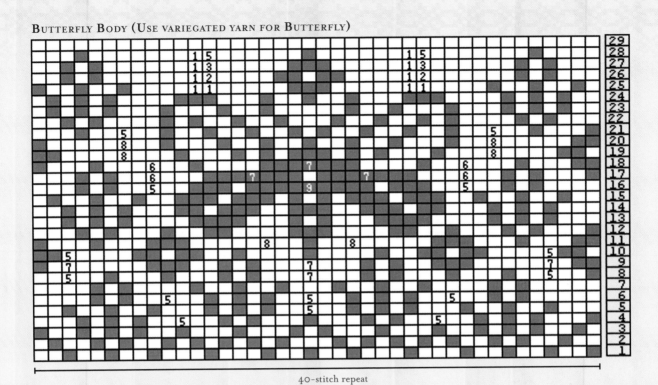

40-stitch repeat

BUTTERFLY SKI HAT CROWN

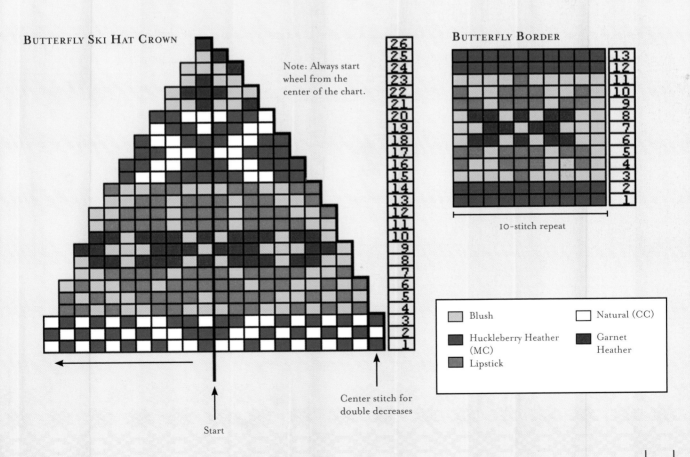

Note: Always start wheel from the center of the chart.

Start

Center stitch for double decreases

BUTTERFLY BORDER

10-stitch repeat

	Blush		Natural (CC)
	Huckleberry Heather (MC)		Garnet Heather
	Lipstick		

CARDINAL CHULLO

YARN

I skein each of Knit Picks Palette (100% wool, 1.75oz/50g, 231yd/210m) in Pimento (MC), Teal, Golden Heather, Lipstick and Tidepool Heather

I skein Cascade Heritage Paints (wool/nylon blend, 3.5oz/100g, 437yd/398m) in color 9883 (variegated)

I skein Knit Picks Bare Superwash Merino, Nylon, Donegal Sock (wool/nylon/Donegal blend, 3.5oz/100g, 462yd/420m) in Natural (CC)

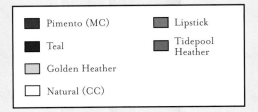

- ■ Pimento (MC)
- ■ Teal
- ☐ Golden Heather
- ☐ Natural (CC)
- ■ Lipstick
- ■ Tidepool Heather

Garter   Garter

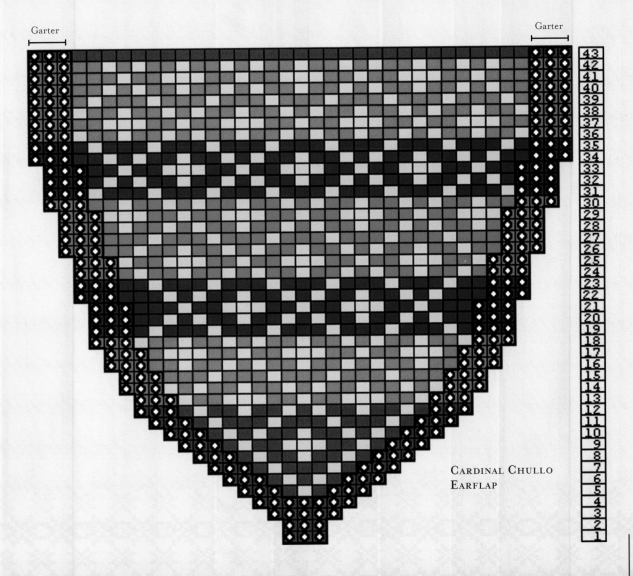

CARDINAL CHULLO
EARFLAP

CARDINAL BORDER

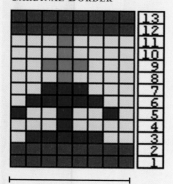

13
12
11
10
9
8
7
6
5
4
3
2
1

8-stitch repeat

CARDINAL CHULLO CROWN

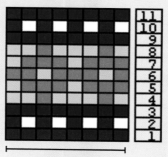

11
10
9
8
7
6
5
4
3
2
1

8-stitch repeat

CARDINAL BODY

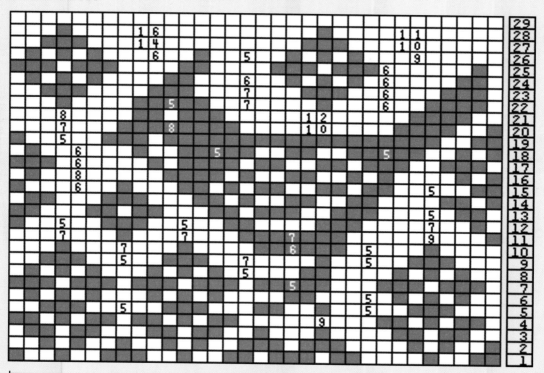

32-stitch repeat

CARDINAL SKI HAT

YARN

1 skein each of Knit Picks Palette (100% wool, 1.75oz/50g, 231yd/210m) in Pimento (MC), Teal, Golden Heather, Lipstick and Tidepool Heather

1 skein Cascade Heritage Paints (wool/nylon blend, 3.5oz/100g, 437yd/398m) in color #9883 (variegated)

1 skein Knit Picks Bare Superwash Merino, Nylon, Donegal Sock (wool/silk blend, 3.5oz/100g, 462yd/420m) in Natural (CC)

CARDINAL SKI HAT CROWN

Note: Always start wheel from the center of the chart.

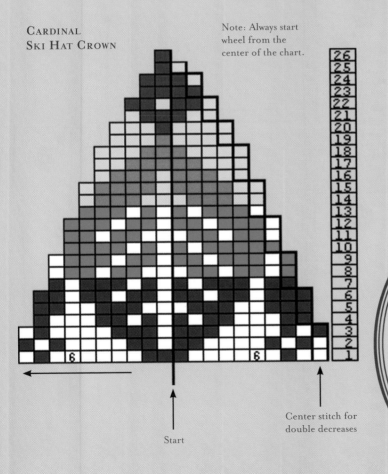

Start

Center stitch for double decreases

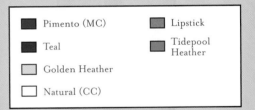

■ Pimento (MC)	■ Lipstick
■ Teal	■ Tidepool Heather
☐ Golden Heather	
☐ Natural (CC)	

CROWN SHAPING FOR CARDINAL SKI HAT

Before beginning crown, knit 2 rnds in CC—160 sts.

All decreases except Rnd 26: Sl 2, k1, p2sso.

Rnd 26 decreases: K2tog tbl.

CHICKADEE CHULLO

YARN

1 skein Knit Picks Stroll Sock (wool/nylon blend, 1.75oz/50g, 231yd/210m) in Black (MC)

1 skein each of Knit Picks Palette (100% wool, 1.75oz/50g, 231yd/210m) in Lipstick, Raspberry Heather and Golden Heather

1 skein Cascade Heritage Paints (wool/nylon blend, 3.5oz/100g, 437yd/398m) in color 9883 (variegated)

1 skein The Alpaca Yarn Company Classic Lite (100% alpaca, 1.75oz/50g, 182yd/166m) in Boston Beige

1 skein Knit Picks Bare Peruvian Highland Wool Fingering (100% wool, 3.5oz/100g, 440yd/400m) in Natural (CC)

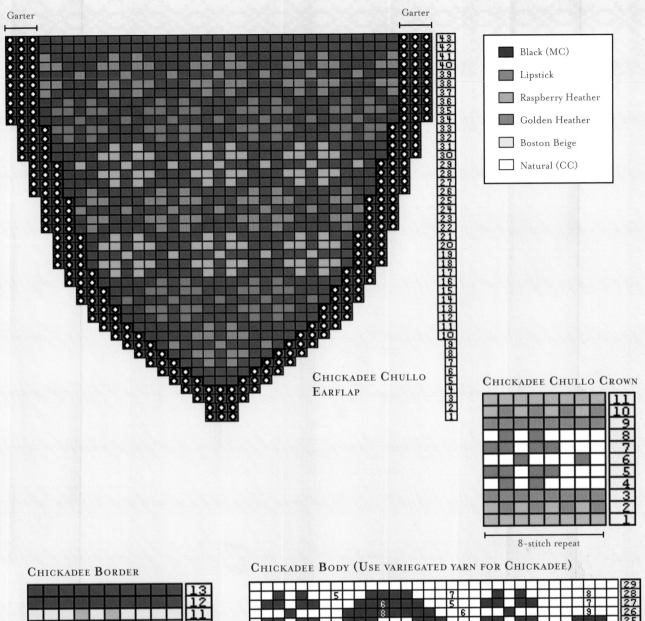

Garter
Garter

CHICKADEE CHULLO
EARFLAP

	Black (MC)
	Lipstick
	Raspberry Heather
	Golden Heather
	Boston Beige
	Natural (CC)

CHICKADEE CHULLO CROWN

8-stitch repeat

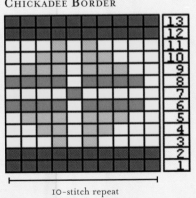

CHICKADEE BORDER

10-stitch repeat

CHICKADEE BODY (USE VARIEGATED YARN FOR CHICKADEE)

32-stitch repeat

Cinnamon Teal Ski Hat

YARN

1 skein each of Knit Picks Palette (100% wool, 1.75oz/50g, 231yd/210m) in Autumn Heather (MC), Garnet Heather, Merlot Heather, Raspberry Heather and Golden Heather

1 skein Crystal Palace Mini Mochi (wool/nylon blend, 1.75oz/50g, 195yd/177m) in color 107 (variegated)

1 skein Knit Picks Bare Merino Wool Sock (100% wool, 3.5oz/100g, 440yd/400mm) in Natural (CC)

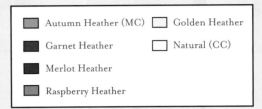

- Autumn Heather (MC)
- Garnet Heather
- Merlot Heather
- Raspberry Heather
- Golden Heather
- Natural (CC)

CINNAMON TEAL BORDER

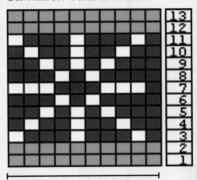

10-stitch repeat

CINNAMON TEAL BODY (USE VARIEGATED YARN FOR CINNAMON TEAL)

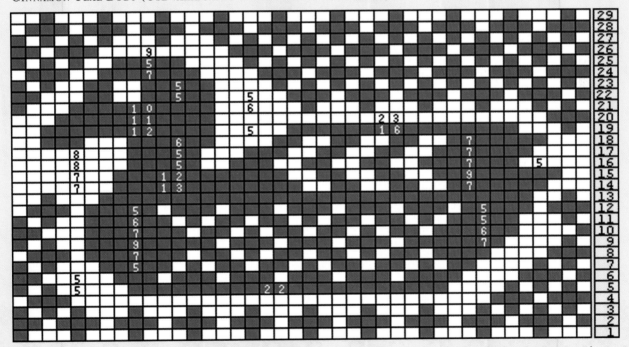

40-stitch repeat

CINNAMON TEAL SKI HAT CROWN

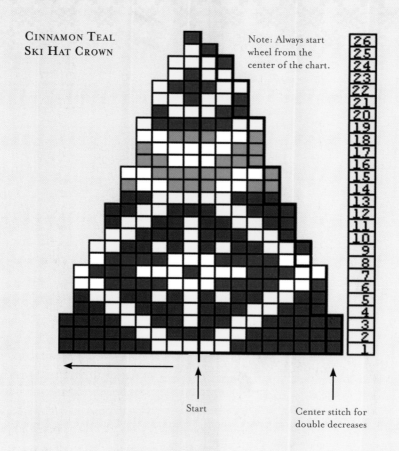

Note: Always start wheel from the center of the chart.

| 26 |
| 25 |
| 24 |
| 23 |
| 22 |
| 21 |
| 20 |
| 19 |
| 18 |
| 17 |
| 16 |
| 15 |
| 14 |
| 13 |
| 12 |
| 11 |
| 10 |
| 9 |
| 8 |
| 7 |
| 6 |
| 5 |
| 4 |
| 3 |
| 2 |
| 1 |

Start

Center stitch for double decreases

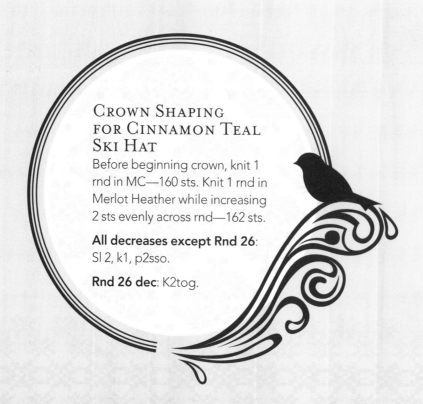

CROWN SHAPING FOR CINNAMON TEAL SKI HAT

Before beginning crown, knit 1 rnd in MC—160 sts. Knit 1 rnd in Merlot Heather while increasing 2 sts evenly across rnd—162 sts.

All decreases except Rnd 26: Sl 2, k1, p2sso.

Rnd 26 dec: K2tog.

CINNAMON TEAL CHULLO

YARN

1 skein each of Knit Picks Palette (100% wool, 1.75oz/50g, 231yd/210m) in Autumn Heather (MC), Garnet Heather, Merlot Heather, Raspberry Heather and Golden Heather

1 skein Crystal Palace Mini Mochi (wool/nylon blend, 1.75oz/50g, 195yd/177m) in color 107 (variegated)

1 skein Knit Picks Bare Merino Wool Sock (100% wool, 3.5oz/100g, 440yd/400mm) in Natural (CC)

CINNAMON TEAL CHULLO EARFLAP

Garter   Garter

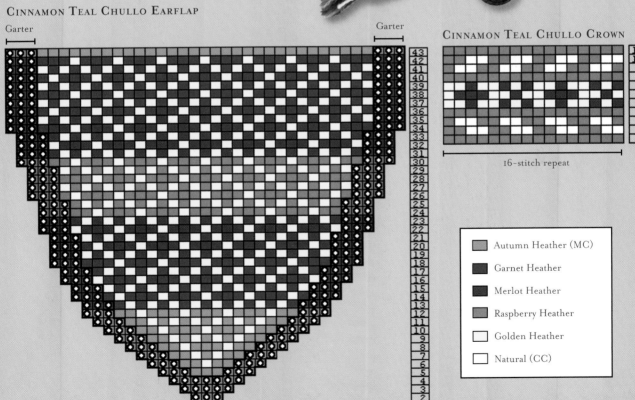

CINNAMON TEAL CHULLO CROWN

16-stitch repeat

	Autumn Heather (MC)
	Garnet Heather
	Merlot Heather
	Raspberry Heather
	Golden Heather
	Natural (CC)

GRIFFIN SKI HAT

YARN

1 skein each of Knit Picks Palette (100% wool, 1.75oz/50g, 231yd/210m) in Blue Note Heather (MC), Blue, Ivy, Rainforest Heather and Celadon Heather

1 skein Knit Picks Imagination Hand Painted Sock (wool/alpaca/nylon blend, 1.75oz/50g, 219yd/199m) in Wicked Witch (variegated)

1 skein Knit Picks Bare Merino Wool, Silk Sock (wool/silk blend, 3.5oz/100g, 440yd/400m) in Natural (CC)

CROWN SHAPING FOR GRIFFIN SKI HAT

Before beginning crown, knit 1 rnd in CC—160 sts. Knit 1 rnd in CC while decreasing 6 sts evenly across rnd—154 sts.

All decreases except Rnd 26: Sl 2, k1, p2sso.

Rnd 26 dec: K2tog tbl.

GRIFFIN BODY (USE VARIEGATED YARN FOR GRIFFIN)

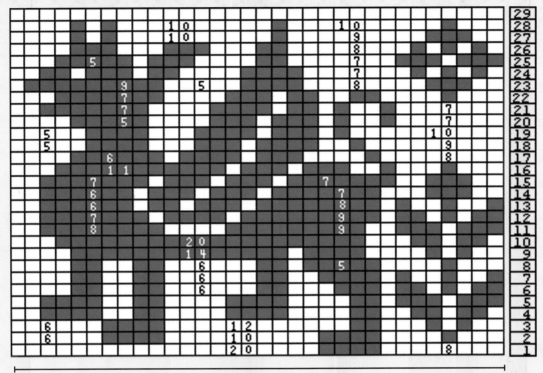

32-stitch repeat

GRIFFIN SKI HAT CROWN

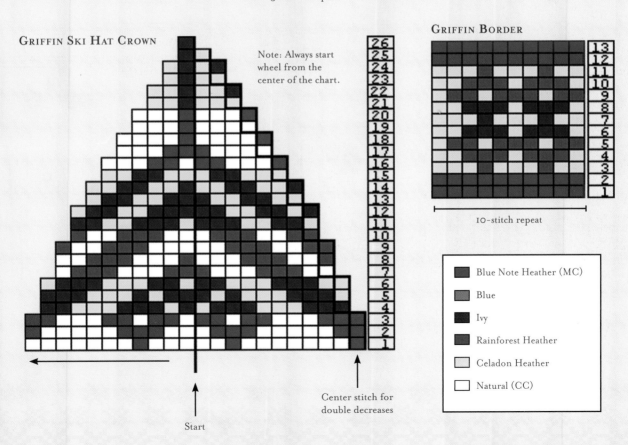

Note: Always start wheel from the center of the chart.

Start

Center stitch for double decreases

GRIFFIN BORDER

10-stitch repeat

- ▅ Blue Note Heather (MC)
- ▅ Blue
- ▅ Ivy
- ▅ Rainforest Heather
- ▅ Celadon Heather
- ☐ Natural (CC)

Grosbeak Ski Hat

YARN

1 skein each of Knit Picks Palette (100% wool, 1.75oz/50g, 231yd/210m) in Garnet Heather (MC), Marine Heather, Black and Oyster Heather

1 skein Cascade Heritage Paints (wool/nylon blend, 3.5oz/100g, 437yd/398m) in color 9928 (variegated)

1 skein Knit Picks Bare Merino Wool Sock (100% wool, 3.5oz/100g, 440yd/400m) in Natural

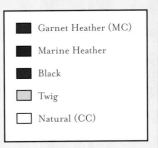

Garnet Heather (MC)

Marine Heather

Black

Twig

Natural (CC)

GROSBEAK BORDER

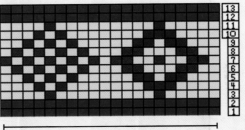

20-stitch repeat

GROSBEAK BODY (USE VARIEGATED YARN FOR GROSBEAK)

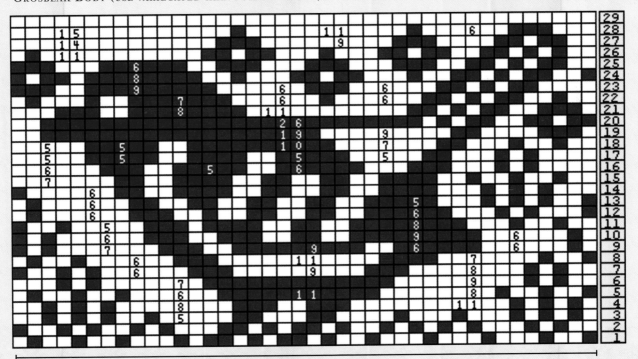

40-stitch repeat

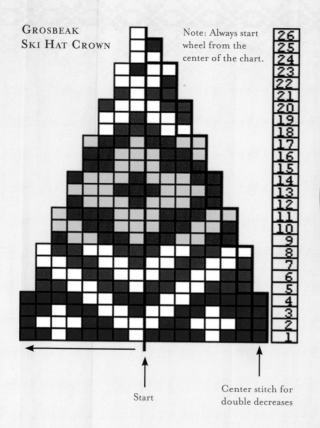

GROSBEAK SKI HAT CROWN

Note: Always start wheel from the center of the chart.

| 26 |
| 25 |
| 24 |
| 23 |
| 22 |
| 21 |
| 20 |
| 19 |
| 18 |
| 17 |
| 16 |
| 15 |
| 14 |
| 13 |
| 12 |
| 11 |
| 10 |
| 9 |
| 8 |
| 7 |
| 6 |
| 5 |
| 4 |
| 3 |
| 2 |
| 1 |

Start

Center stitch for double decreases

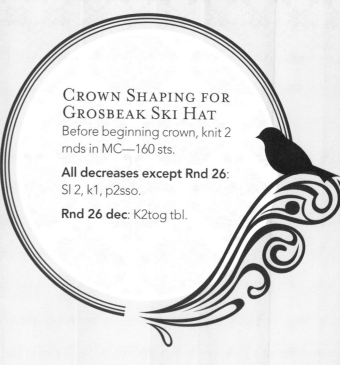

CROWN SHAPING FOR GROSBEAK SKI HAT

Before beginning crown, knit 2 rnds in MC—160 sts.

All decreases except Rnd 26: Sl 2, k1, p2sso.

Rnd 26 dec: K2tog tbl.

❧ *Variation*

GROSBEAK CHULLO

YARN

1 skein each of Knit Picks Palette (100% wool, 1.75oz/50g, 231yd/210m) in Garnet Heather (MC), Marine Heather and Black

1 skein Jamieson & Smith 2-ply Jumper Weight (100% wool, 0.88oz/25g, 125yd/114m) in Dog Rose

1 skein Cascade Heritage Paints (wool/nylon blend, 3.5oz/100g, 437yd/398m) in color 9928 (variegated)

1 skein Knit Picks Bare Merino Wool Sock (100% wool, 3.5oz/100g, 440yd/400m) in Natural (CC)

GROSBEAK CHULLO CROWN

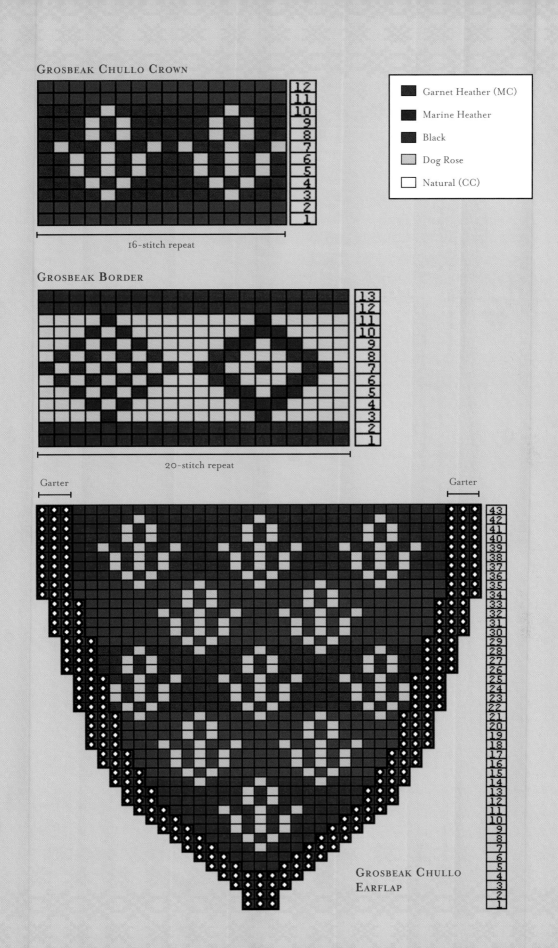

16-stitch repeat

GROSBEAK BORDER

20-stitch repeat

Garter   Garter

Legend

- ■ Garnet Heather (MC)
- ■ Marine Heather
- ■ Black
- ▨ Dog Rose
- ☐ Natural (CC)

GROSBEAK CHULLO
EARFLAP

NUTHATCH SKI HAT

YARN

1 skein each of Knit Picks Palette (100% wool, 1.75oz/50g, 231yd/210m) in Black (MC), Asphalt Heather, Marble Heather, Mist and Marine Heather

1 skein Zitron Trekking XXL (wool/nylon blend, 3.5oz/100g, 459yd/418m) in color 185 (variegated)

1 skein Knit Picks Bare Peruvian Highland Wool Fingering (100% wool, 3.5oz/100g, 440yd/400m) in Natural (CC)

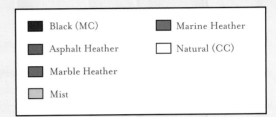

Legend:
- ■ Black (MC)
- ■ Asphalt Heather
- ■ Marble Heather
- ■ Mist
- ■ Marine Heather
- □ Natural (CC)

NUTHATCH BORDER

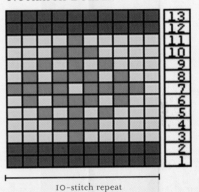

10-stitch repeat

NUTHATCH BODY (USE VARIEGATED YARN FOR NUTHATCH)

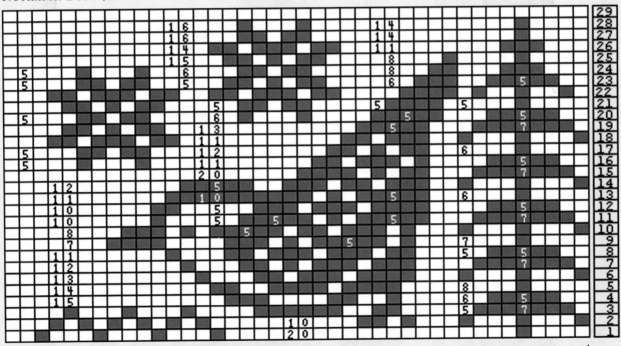

40-stitch repeat

NUTHATCH
SKI HAT CROWN

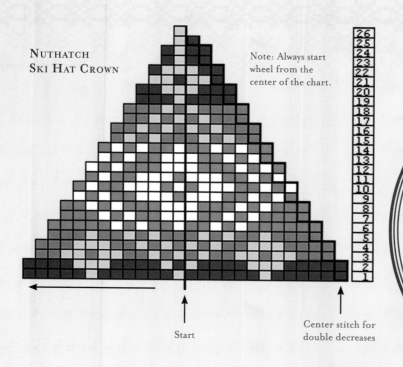

Note: Always start wheel from the center of the chart.

26
25
24
23
22
21
20
19
18
17
16
15
14
13
12
11
10
9
8
7
6
5
4
3
2
1

Start

Center stitch for double decreases

CROWN SHAPING FOR NUTHATCH SKI HAT

Before beginning crown, knit 1 rnd in MC—160 sts. Knit 1 rnd in MC while decreasing 4 sts evenly across rnd—156 sts.

All decreases except Rnd 26: Sl 2, k1, p2sso.

Rnd 26 dec: K2tog tbl.

❧ *Variation*

NUTHATCH CHULLO

YARN

1 skein each of Knit Picks Palette (100% wool, 1.75oz/50g, 231yd/210m) in Black (MC), Asphalt Heather, Marble Heather, Mist and Marine Heather

1 skein Zitron Trekking XXL (wool/nylon blend, 3.5oz/100g, 459yd/418m) in color 185 (variegated)

1 skein Knit Picks Bare Peruvian Highland Wool Fingering (100% wool, 3.5oz/100g, 440yd/400m) in Natural (CC)

Nuthatch Chullo Crown

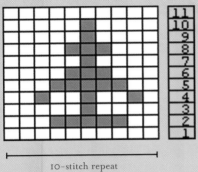

10-stitch repeat

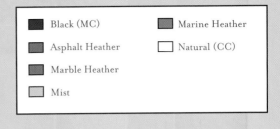

■	Black (MC)
■	Asphalt Heather
■	Marble Heather
□	Mist
■	Marine Heather
□	Natural (CC)

Garter   Garter

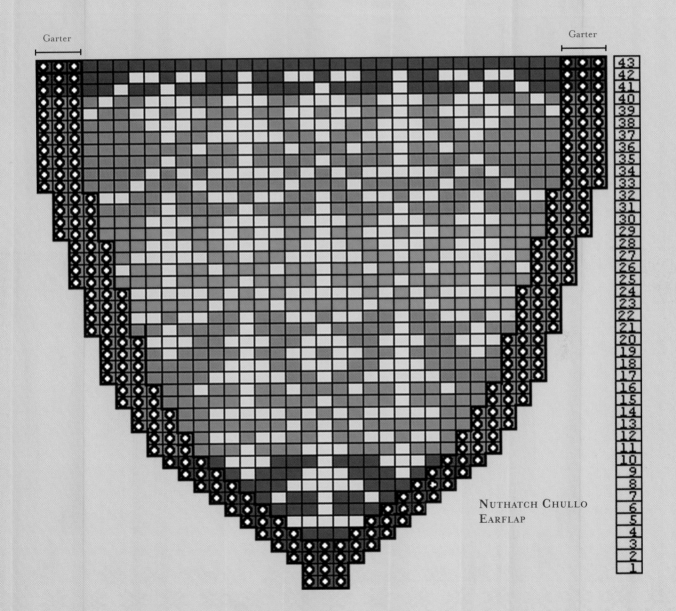

Nuthatch Chullo
Earflap

REINDEER SKI HAT

YARN

1 skein each of Knit Picks Palette (100% wool, 1.75oz/50g, 231yd/210m) in Merlot Heather (MC), Oyster Heather, Brindle Heather and Garnet Heather

1 skein Zitron Trekking XXL (wool/nylon blend, 3.5oz/100g, 459yd/418m) in color 183 (variegated)

1 skein Knit Picks Bare Merino Wool Sock (100% wool, 3.5oz/100g, 440yd/400m) in Natural (CC)

CROWN SHAPING FOR REINDEER SKI HAT

Before beginning crown, knit 1 rnd in Oyster Heather—160 sts. Knit 1 rnd in Oyster Heather while decreasing 4 sts evenly across rnd—156 sts.

All decreases except Rnd 26: Sl 2, k1, p2sso.

Rnd 26 dec: K2tog tbl.

REINDEER BODY (USE VARIEGATED YARN FOR REINDEER)

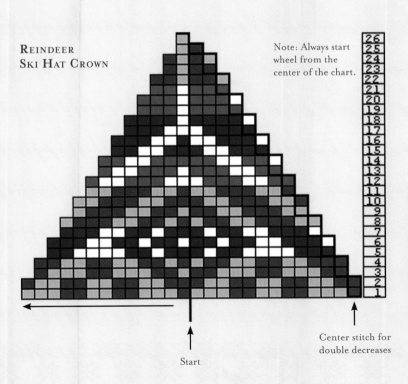

32-stitch repeat

REINDEER SKI HAT CROWN

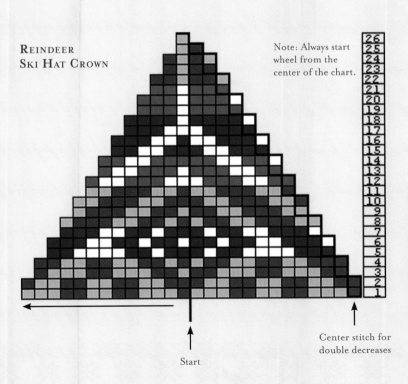

Note: Always start wheel from the center of the chart.

Start

Center stitch for double decreases

■	Oyster Heather
■	Brindle Heather
■	Garnet Heather
■	Merlot Heather (MC)
□	Natural (CC)

REINDEER BORDER

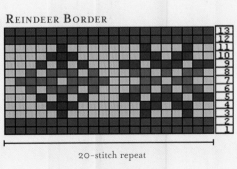

20-stitch repeat

WOOD DUCK CHULLO

YARN

1 skein each of Knit Picks
Palette (100% wool,
1.75oz/50g, 231yd/210m) in
Ivy (MC), Eggplant, Oyster
Heather, Marine Heather
and Garnet Heather

1 skein Cascade Heritage
Paints (wool/nylon blend,
3.5oz/100g, 437yd/398m) in
color 9826 (variegated)

1 skein Knit Picks Bare
Peruvian Highland Wool
Fingering (100% wool,
3.5oz/100g, 440yd/400m)
in Natural (CC)

◼	Eggplant
◻	Oyster Heather
◼	Marine Heather
◼	Garnet Heather
◼	Ivy (MC)
◻	Natural (CC)

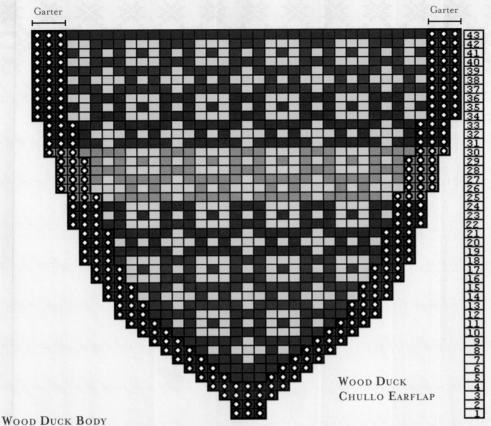

**WOOD DUCK
CHULLO EARFLAP**

Garter

WOOD DUCK BODY
(USE VARIEGATED YARN FOR WOOD DUCK)

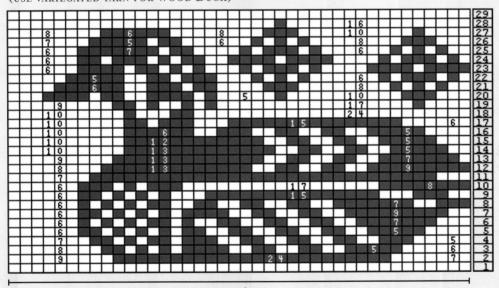

40-stitch repeat

WOOD DUCK BORDER

20-stitch repeat

WOOD DUCK CHULLO CROWN

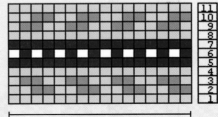

16-stitch repeat

SIX-POINT LEAF AND FLOWER TAM

YARN

1 skein each of Jamieson & Smith Spindrift (100% wool, 0.88oz/25g, 115yd/105m) in Port Wine, Sunrise, Raspberry, Peach and Wild Violet

1 skein Jamieson & Smith 2 Ply Jumper Weight (100% wool, 0.88oz/25g, 125yd/114m) in Salmon

- Port Wine
- Sunrise
- Raspberry
- Peach
- Salmon
- Wild Violet

Tam Brim and Top

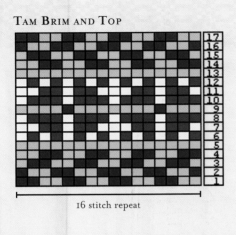

17 16 15 14 13 12 11 10 9 8 7 6 5 4 3 2 1

16 stitch repeat

Tam Wheel

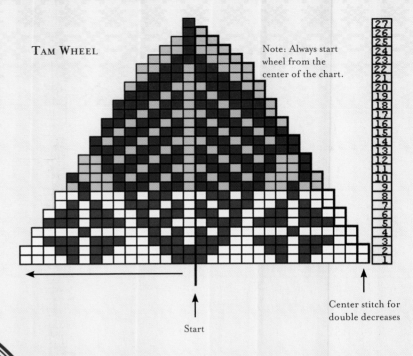

Note: Always start wheel from the center of the chart.

27 26 25 24 23 22 21 20 19 18 17 16 15 14 13 12 11 10 9 8 7 6 5 4 3 2 1

Center stitch for double decreases

Start

CORRUGATED RIBBING PATTERN

Rnds 1–3: *K2 in Sunrise, p2 in Wild Violet; rep from * around.

Rnds 4–5: *K2 in Port Wine, p2 in Salmon; rep from * around.

Rnds 6–8: *K2 in Raspberry, p2 in Peach; rep from * around.

Rnds 9–10: *K2 in Port Wine, p2 in Salmon; rep from * around.

TAM

Using Sunrise, cast on 144 sts and divide evenly onto 3 needles—48 sts on each needle. Foll Corrugated Ribbing patt for 13 rnds.

Knit 1 rnd in Salmon while increasing 10 sts evenly on the first needle, 12 sts evenly on the second needle and 10 sts evenly on the third needle—176 sts.

BRIM

Work Rnds 1–17 of the Tam Brim and Top chart.

Knit 1 rnd in Salmon.

TOP

Work Rnds 1–17 of the Tam Brim and Top chart.

Knit 1 rnd of Peach while increasing 4 sts evenly across rnd—180 sts.

TAM WHEEL

Work Tam Wheel chart.

Note: This patt uses a 30-stitch repeat, which produces a 6-point wheel. It may be helpful to switch to 8" (20cm) dpns as the number of sts decreases.

All decreases (except those on Rnds 11 and 27): Sl 2 as if to knit, k1, p2sso.

Rnd 11 dec: Sl 1, k2tog, psso.

Rnd 27 dec: K2tog tbl with Raspberry.

After the last dec, 6 sts rem. Cut yarn and draw the tail through rem sts. Weave in all ends and block.

Six-Point Snowflake Medallion Tam

YARN

1 skein each of Jamieson & Smith Spindrift (100% wool, 0.88oz/25g, 115yd/105m) in Mulberry, Blueberry, Salmon, Wild Violet and Sand

1 skein Jamieson & Smith 2 Ply Jumper Weight (100% wool, 0.88oz/25g, 125yd/114m) in Garnet

■	Mulberry
■	Blueberry
■	Garnet
■	Salmon
■	Wild Violet
■	Sand

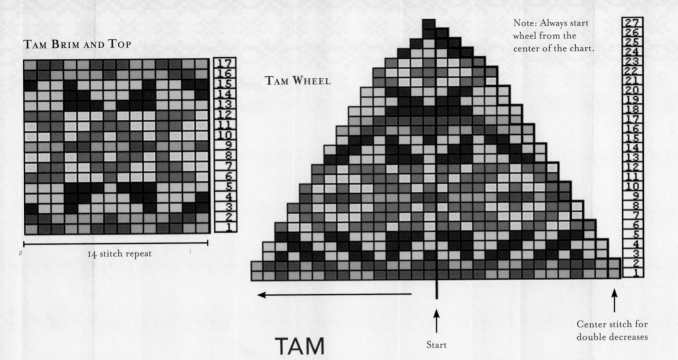

Tam Brim and Top

14 stitch repeat

Tam Wheel

Note: Always start wheel from the center of the chart.

Start

Center stitch for double decreases

TAM

Using Mulberry, cast on 144 sts and divide evenly onto 3 needles— 48 sts on each needle. Foll Corrugated Ribbing patt for 13 rnds.

Knit 1 rnd in Salmon while increasing 13 sts evenly on the first needle, 12 sts evenly on the second needle and 13 sts evenly on the third needle—182 sts.

BRIM

Work Rnds 1–17 of the Tam Brim and Top chart.

Knit 1 rnd in Salmon.

TOP

Work Rnds 1–17 of the Tam Brim and Top chart.

Knit 1 rnd of Salmon while decreasing 2 sts evenly across rnd—180 sts.

TAM WHEEL

Work Tam Wheel chart.

Note: This patt uses a 30-stitch repeat, which produces a 6-point wheel. It may be helpful to switch to 8" (20cm) dpns as the number of sts decreases.

All decreases (except those on Rnds 9 and 27): Sl 2 as if to knit, k1, p2sso.

Rnd 9 dec: Sl 1, k2tog, psso.

Rnd 27 dec: K2tog tbl with Blueberry.

After the last dec, 6 sts rem. Cut yarn and draw the tail through rem sts. Weave in all ends and block.

CORRUGATED RIBBING PATTERN

Rnds 1–3: *K2 in Mulberry, p2 in Salmon; rep from * around.

Rnds 4–5: *K2 in Blueberry, p2 in Wild Violet; rep from * around.

Rnds 6–8: *K2 in Garnet, p2 in Sand; rep from * around.

Rnds 9–10: *K2 in Blueberry, p2 in Wild Violet; rep from * around.

Rnds 11–13: *K2 in Mulberry, p2 in Salmon; rep from * around.

SEVEN-POINT STAR TAM

YARN

1 skein each of Yarns International Shetland Supreme (100% wool, 1.75oz/50g, 190yd/173m) in Shetland Black, Moorit, Gaulmogot and Shetland White

1 skein each of Jamieson & Smith Spindrift (100% wool, 0.88oz/25g, 115yd/105m) in Sunrise and Wild Violet

■	Shetland Black
■	Moorit
■	Sunrise
■	Wild Violet
■	Gaulmogot
□	Shetland White

TAM BRIM AND TOP

12 stitch repeat

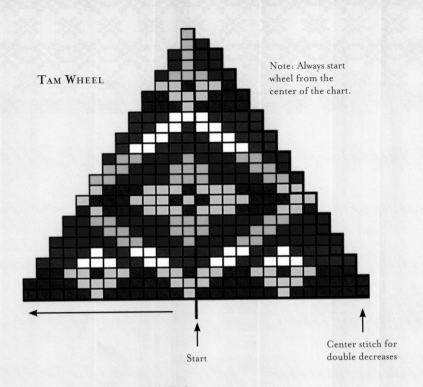

TAM WHEEL

Note: Always start wheel from the center of the chart.

Start

Center stitch for double decreases

TAM

Using Shetland Black, cast on 144 sts and divide evenly onto 3 needles (48 sts on each needle). Foll Corrugated Ribbing patt for 13 rnds.

Knit 1 rnd in Sunrise while increasing 12 sts evenly on each needle—180 sts.

BRIM
Work Rnds 1–17 of the Tam Brim and Top chart.

Knit 1 rnd in Sunrise.

TOP
Work Rnds 1–17 of the Tam Brim and Top chart.

Knit 1 rnd in Sunrise while increasing 2 sts evenly across rnd—182 sts.

TAM WHEEL
Work Tam Wheel chart.

Note: This patt uses a 26-stitch repeat, which produces a 7-point wheel. It may be helpful to switch to the 8" (20cm) dpns as the number of sts decreases.

All decreases (except those on Rnd 26): Sl 2 as if to knit, k1, p2sso.

Rnd 26 dec: K2tog tbl with Wild Violet.

After the last dec, 7 sts rem. Cut yarn and draw the tail through rem sts. Weave in all ends and block.

CORRUGATED RIBBING PATTERN

Rnds 1–3: *K2 in Shetland Black, p2 in Gaulmogot; rep from * around.

Rnds 4–5: *K2 in Moorit, p2 in Shetland White; rep from * around.

Rnds 6–8: *K2 in Sunrise, p2 in Wild Violet; rep from * around.

Rnds 9–10: *K2 in Moorit, p2 in Shetland White; rep from * around.

Rnds 11–13: *K2 in Shetland Black, p2 in Gaulmogot; rep from * around.

THIRTEEN-POINT ALLOVER TAM

YARN

1 skein each of Yarns International Shetland Supreme (100% wool, 1.75oz/50g, 190yd/173m) in Shetland Black, Yuglet, Moorit, Gaulmogot, Mooskit and Shetland White

■	Black
■	Yuglet
■	Moorit
□	Gaulmogot
□	Mooskit
□	White

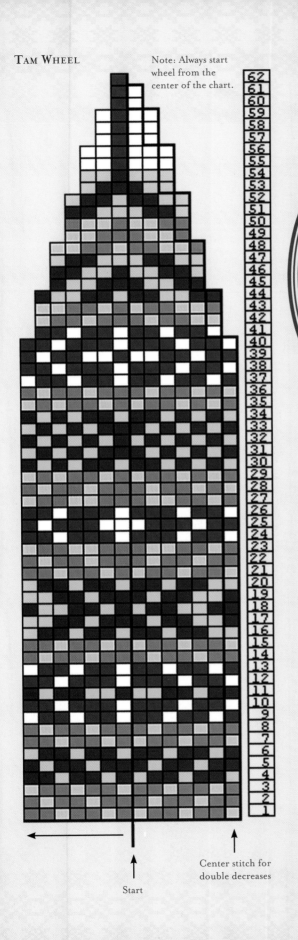

TAM WHEEL

Note: Always start wheel from the center of the chart.

Start

Center stitch for double decreases

CORRUGATED RIBBING PATTERN

Rnds 1–3: *K2 in Shetland Black, p2 in Gaulmogot; rep from * around.

Rnds 4–5: *K2 in Yuglet, p2 in Mooskit; rep from * around.

Rnds 6–8: *K2 in Moorit, p2 in Shetland White; rep from * around.

Rnds 9–10: *K2 in Yuglet, p2 in Mooskit; rep from * around.

Rnds 11–13: *K2 in Shetland Black, p2 in Gaulmogot; rep from * around.

TAM

Using Shetland Black, cast on 144 sts and divide evenly onto 3 needles—48 sts on each needle. Foll Corrugated Ribbing patt for 13 rnds.

Knit 1 rnd in Gaulmogot while increasing 13 sts evenly on the first and third needles and 12 sts evenly on the second needle—182 sts.

Work Rnds 1–62 of the Tam Wheel chart.

Note: It may be helpful to switch to the 8" (20cm) dpns as the number of sts decreases.

All decreases (except those on Rnd 62): Sl 2 as if to knit, k1, p2sso.

Rnd 62 dec: K2tog tbl with Moorit.

After the last dec, 13 sts rem. Cut yarn and draw the tail through rem sts. Weave in all ends and block.

CHAPTER TWO
MITTENS

In the next section, you will find complete directions and charts to knit exquisite and charming mittens. I have constructed these mittens using a wide variety of yarns. I especially like the variegated sock yarns since they add dimensionality to the designs.

I fondly remember knitting my first pair of mittens under my grandmother's tutelage. I loved everything about knitting mittens except making the thumbs. I would knit six or eight pairs of mittens and then spend an evening knitting the thumbs. It was my way of lessening this unpleasant experience. Recently, a friend conveyed the story of a mother-daughter team making mittens during a craft sale. Stacked upon their table were several pairs of mittens all lacking the thumbs. They clearly shared my dislike. My attitude toward thumb-knitting changed when I developed designs for crown-to-cuff mittens. With this technique, I knit the thumb first, storing the stitches on safety pins until needed.

I also must admit that I wasn't very fond of the mitten crown decreases because the ever-decreasing number of stitches easily slid off the needles. To finish the mitten, the remaining stitches were drawn through a loop, leaving a visible unknit circle of stitches for all to see. The crowns of the mittens in this book have no apparent closure since they use a Turkish cast on.

I've knit more than one hundred pairs of mittens using the crown-to-cuff technique, and I now love making the thumbs. Of course, beginning at the crown means that the bird or beast designs are written upside down; that is, you begin with the bird or beast's head and work downward to its feet. I actually find it fun to watch the bird or beast emerge against the mitten's background. It is also easier to check a mitten's fit when you begin at the crown.

I hope that you will find crown-to-cuff mitten making as pleasurable as I do. Your first pair will be the most difficult because you're learning a new technique; however, once you've mastered this technique, you should find that you can knit mittens more quickly than previously.

BASIC MITTEN PATTERN

MITTENS

All mittens begin with the thumb, which is knit first and placed on safety pins until needed. Unlike the usual way of knitting mittens, these thumbs have no apparent closure at the top, and you won't have the weight of the mitten body hanging down while you knit the thumb.

Both the mitten body and thumb begin with a Turkish cast on; this is the cast on used for toe-up socks. A two-stitch border of MC stitches separates the palm and back of the hand. After the cast on, knit the salt-and-pepper rounds, which are a simple alteration of dark (MC) and light (CC) stitches. The salt-and-pepper pattern hides the crown increases that occur at each side of the dark border stitches on the mitten back and palm. You can extend or reduce the number of salt-and-pepper rounds to change the length of the mitten.

The palm pattern for all mittens uses a Sanquhar mitten design. If you're knitting a bird or beast mitten, knit the back of the hand using the bird or beast pattern. Otherwise, knit the Sanquhar design for both the palm and back of the mitten. Pay attention to the placement of the bird or beast on the mitten. For the right mitten, the bird or beast pattern is knit on the first 41 stitches, while the Sanquhar design is knit on the last 41 stitches. For the left mitten, the Sanquhar design is knit on the first 41 stitches, while the bird or beast design is knit on the last 41 stitches.

The bird or beast mittens begin and end with a Sanquhar border design. Although the graphs for the bird or beast mittens use a specific Sanquhar mitten design, you may substitute any Sanquhar mitten design that you wish.

The mitten directions indicate when to attach the thumb to the mitten. A 3-Needle bind off secures the palm and inside thumb stitches. Placement of the thumb depends on the right or left mitten.

The mitten ends with 20 rounds of corrugated ribbing, a k2, p2 rib in which the MC is used for the knit stitches and the CC is used for the purl stitches.

CUSTOMIZING THE MITTENS

The finished mittens should fit most women; however, the designs lend themselves well to modification. When knitting the thumb, adjust the number of salt-and-pepper rounds until the mitten thumb barely touches the bottom of the wearer's thumb. You can also adjust the salt-and-pepper rounds until the mitten body reaches the edge of the wearer's thumb.

SIZE

One size fits most women

NEEDLES

One set of 6" (15cm) US 0 (2mm) double-pointed needles

One set of 8" (20cm) US 0 (2mm) double-pointed needles

If necessary, change needle size to obtain correct gauge.

GAUGE

42 sts and 40 rows = 4" (10cm) in St st

MITTENS

THUMB

Note: Each patt has its own left and right thumb chart. Refer to that chart when knitting the mitten thumbs.

Cast on 6 sts and distribute evenly onto 2 needles, using Turkish cast on and MC. Knit across the sts on each needle.

Note: Refer to the thumb chart for the desired Sanquhar patt. Because the first rnd contains a single increase, it is easier to combine Needles 1 and 2 onto the first needle and Needles 3 and 4 onto the second needle. This lessens the possibility of the sts slipping off the ends of the needle.

Thumb Rnd 1 (inc rnd):

First Needle: K3 following Sanquhar thumb chart for Needle 1. M1 following Sanquhar thumb chart for Needle 2.

Second Needle: K3 following Sanquhar thumb chart for Needle 3. M1 following Sanquhar thumb chart for Needle 4—8 sts.

Thumb Rnd 2 (inc rnd):

Needle 1: K3 following Sanquhar thumb chart for Needle 1—1 st rem on LH needle.

Needle 2: With a new needle (Needle 2), incR using MC. Knit next st using CC. IncL using MC.

Needle 3: K3 following Sanquhar thumb chart for Needle 3—1 st rem on LH needle.

Needle 4: IncR using MC. Knit the next st using CC. IncL using MC—12 sts.

Thumb Rnds 3–6 (inc rnds):

Cont to foll Sanquhar thumb chart for desired thumb (right or left), increasing 1 st at each end of Needle 2 and Needle 4 as shown on chart—28 sts after Rnd 6.

Note: Rnd 3 and 4 increases are in the salt-and-pepper patt while Rnd 5 and 6 increases are in the Sanquhar patt.

Thumb Rnds 7–23: Foll Sanquhar thumb chart for desired thumb (right or left).

MITTEN HINTS

Mitten Crown and Thumb

- ❧ Be careful when knitting the cast on stitches because knitting the stitches on the second needle can cause the stitches on the first needle to slip off the end of the needle.
- ❧ The initial three rounds are difficult because you have only a few stitches each on four needles. Once you make it past these rounds, the knitting becomes easier.
- ❧ Although the patterns show four needles in action excluding the needle doing the knitting, I typically only use three for ease in knitting. Feel free to divide the stitches as you see fit.
- ❧ After Round 10 you may wish to weave the cast on yarn tail to the inside of the crown or thumb. This not only gets the yarn out of your way, it saves you time later.

Minimizing Holes Around the Thumbs

You will notice a gap on each side where the thumb joins the mitten body. Slip the stitch before the gap. Pick up the left and right stitches one round before the gap. Knit these two stitches together. Pass the slipped stitch over the stitches knit together. (Essentially, this is a sl 1, k2tog, psso.) Do this for each side of the thumb. Any remaining gaps will be very small, and you can use the tails remaining from the 3-Needle bind off to close them.

Thumb Rnd 24: Knit to last st of rnd following Sanquhar thumb chart. Place last st of Needle 4 onto Needle 1. Place first st of Needle 4 onto Needle 3. Purl across rem 9 sts on Needle 4 using MC. Place these 9 inside thumb sts on a safety pin. Divide the 19 rem sts between 2 safety pins. Cut yarns, leaving long tails. Set the thumb aside until you reach Rnd 48 of the mitten body.

MITTEN BODY

Cast on 18 sts and distribute evenly on 2 needles, using Eastern cast on and the 6" (15cm) needles. Knit across sts on each needle.

Note: The mitten designs for the back of the hand and the palm are identical on Rnds 1–17. Both use the salt-and-pepper patt to conceal the crown increases.

Rnd 1: There are no increases on the first rnd. Knit the sts on the first cast-on needle following the salt-and-pepper patt from the body chart. Knit 5 sts from the second cast-on needle (Needle 2) following the salt-and-pepper patt. With a new needle (Needle 3), knit the remaining sts from the second cast-on needle following the salt-and-pepper pattern.

Rnds 2–17 (inc rnds): Knit the first st in MC. IncR with CC. Foll salt-and-pepper patt to the last st. IncL using CC. Knit the last st in MC. Rep for second side of mitten—82 sts after Rnd 17.

Note: Switch to 8" (20cm) dpns when the sts become cramped.

Rnds 18–47:

RIGHT MITTEN: Foll bird or beast body chart for the first 41 sts and Sanquhar body chart for the last 41 sts.

LEFT MITTEN: Foll Sanquhar body chart for the first 41 sts and bird or beast body chart for the last 41 sts.

ATTACH THUMB

Rnd 48: This corresponds to the solid dark line (MC) beginning the fourth Sanquhar patt.

Note: The thumb gusset replaces the last Sanquhar box on the right mitten and the first Sanquhar box on the left mitten. No additional sts are cast on for the thumb.

RIGHT THUMB: Knit the back of the hand using bird or beast body chart. Knit palm using Sanquhar body chart; end with stitch 31—1 Sanquhar box and 10 sts rem on needle. Remove inside thumb sts from holder and place on a needle. Use 3-Needle bind off to bind off the next 9 palm sts with the 9 inside thumb sts. Place rem thumb sts onto the needle. Knit these sts following right thumb gusset chart. Knit the last st in MC.

LEFT THUMB: Remove the 9 inside thumb sts from holder and place on a needle. Knit the first st in MC, then use 3-Needle bind off to bind off the next 9 palm sts with the 9 inside thumb sts. Place rem thumb sts onto the needle. Knit these sts following the left thumb gusset chart. Knit the palm sts following the Sanquhar body chart, starting at stitch 11 (beginning of the second Sanquhar box). Knit the back of the hand using the bird or beast body chart.

Rnds 49-65: Foll the bird or beast body chart, the Sanquhar body chart and the thumb chart as dictated by your chosen design.

AT THE SAME TIME:

Rnd 52: Work the thumb gusset dec as k1, sl 1, k1 (CC), psso. Work in patt to last 3 sts, k2tog (CC), k1. This maintains the white border stripe for 5 rnds.

Cont to foll Sanquhar body chart, bird or beast chart and thumb chart as directed for the right and left mittens through Rnd 65.

Rnd 66 (last thumb dec): Sl 1, k2tog, psso.

Cont to foll the bird or beast body chart and the Sanquhar body chart as directed for the right and left mittens.

Rnds 67–69: Cont to foll the bird or beast body chart and the Sanquhar body chart as directed for the right and left mittens—74 sts after Rnd 69.

CUFF

Work 20 rnds of corrugated ribbing (k2 MC, p2 CC), decreasing 6 sts evenly across the first rnd—68 sts. Bind off in MC. Weave in all ends and block.

Options for Mittens

Sanquhar Mittens

I began making crown-to-cuff mittens using only the Sanquhar body chart. These mittens are beautiful even without the bird or beast designs and are a good starting mitten for learning the crown-to-cuff technique. To make these mittens, simply knit the Sanquhar body chart for both the palm and back of the hand.

Bird or Beast Mittens Using a Different Sanquhar Body Chart

To make bird or beast mittens with a different Sanquhar design, follow the thumb directions for the Sanquhar body chart of your choice. Follow the directions for the bird or beast mittens, substituting your desired Sanquhar body chart for the palm. For the top and bottom borders on the back of the hand, substitute Rounds 18–28 of your selected Sanquhar body chart for Rounds 18–28 of the bird or beast mitten design, and substitute Rounds 58-69 of the Sanquhar body chart for Rounds 58-69 of the bird or beast body chart. This substitution replaces the top and bottom Sanquhar borders with your selected design.

BUTTERFLY MITTENS

YARN

1 skein Knit Picks Imagination Hand Painted Sock (wool/alpaca/nylon blend, 1.75oz/50g, 219yd/199m) in Damsel (MC)

1 skein Knit Picks Bare Merino Wool, Silk Sock (wool/silk blend, 3.5oz/100g, 440yd/400m) in Natural (CC)

Note: In the mitten charts, the darker color is MC and the lighter color is CC.

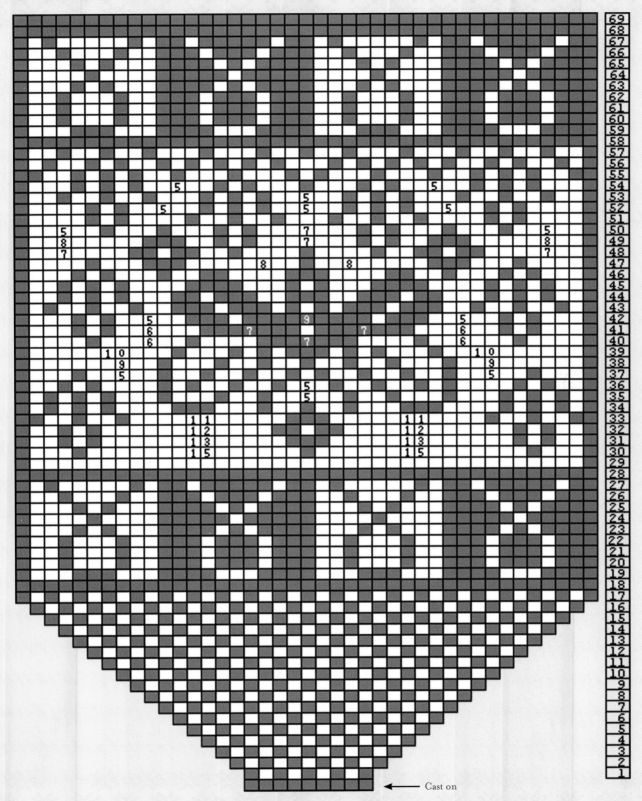

Cast on

Cancer Survivor Body

Butterfly Mittens: Use for Palm.
Sanquhar Mittens: Use for Palm and Back of Hand.

← Cast On

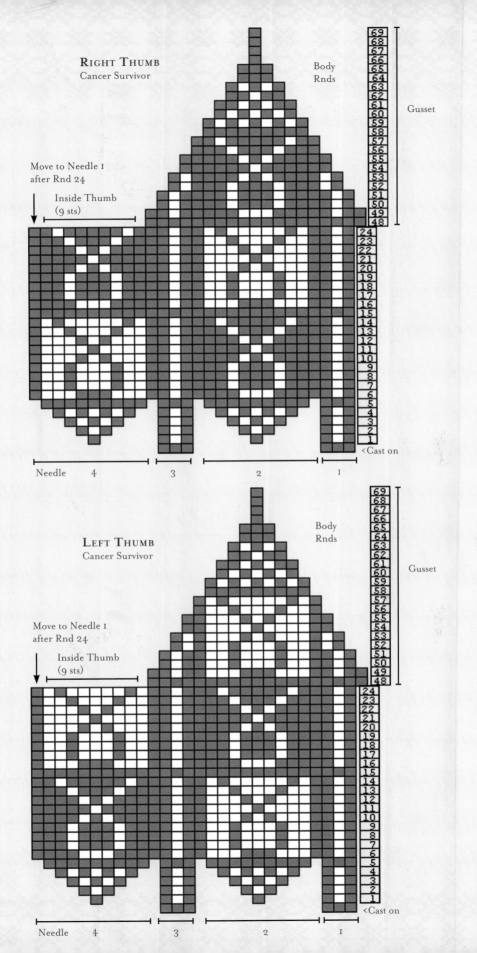

RIGHT THUMB
Cancer Survivor

Body
Rnds

Gusset

Move to Needle 1
after Rnd 24

Inside Thumb
(9 sts)

Needle 4   3   2   1

< Cast on

LEFT THUMB
Cancer Survivor

Body
Rnds

Gusset

Move to Needle 1
after Rnd 24

Inside Thumb
(9 sts)

Needle 4   3   2   1

< Cast on

CARDINAL MITTENS

YARN

1 skein Indiecita Baby Alpaca DK (100% alpaca, 1.75oz/50g, 125yd/114m) in color 2060 (MC)

1 skein Knitpicks Bare Superwash Merino, Nylon, Donegal Sock (wool/nylon/Donegal blend, 3.5oz/100g, 462yd/420m) in Natural (CC)

Note: In the mitten charts, the darker color is MC and the lighter color is CC.

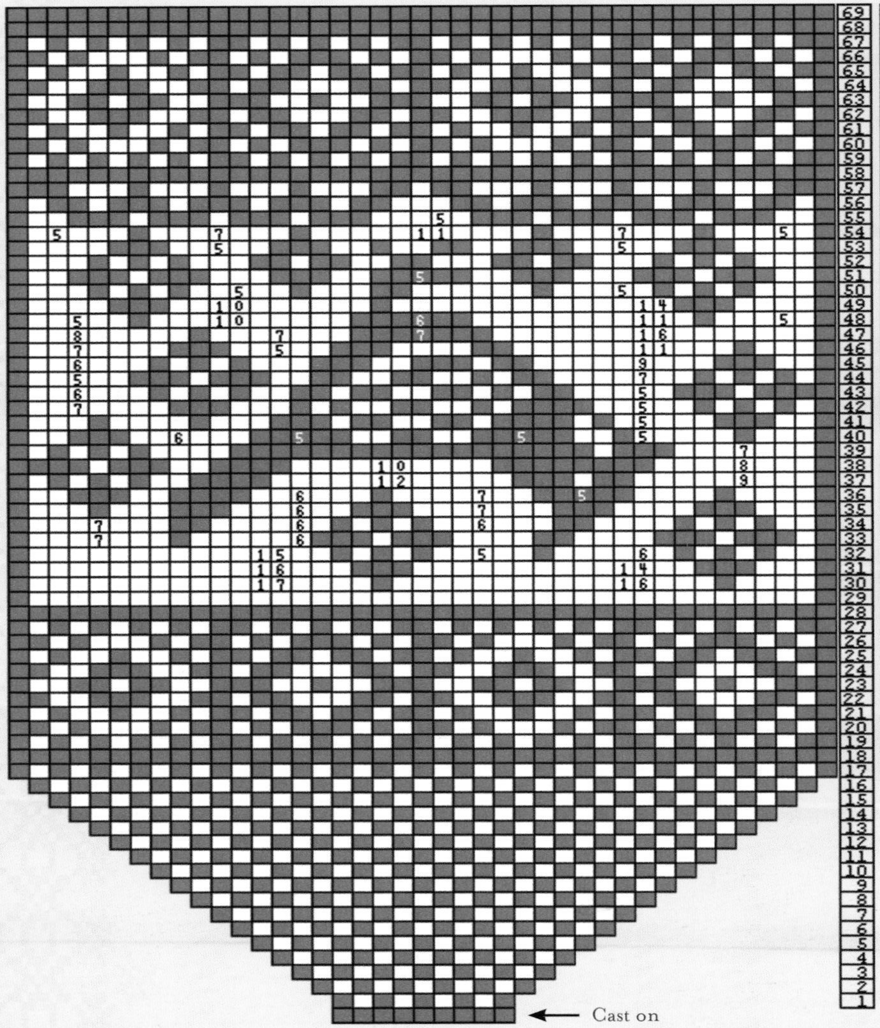

Left Cardinal Body

Right Cardinal Body

Cast on

Cast on

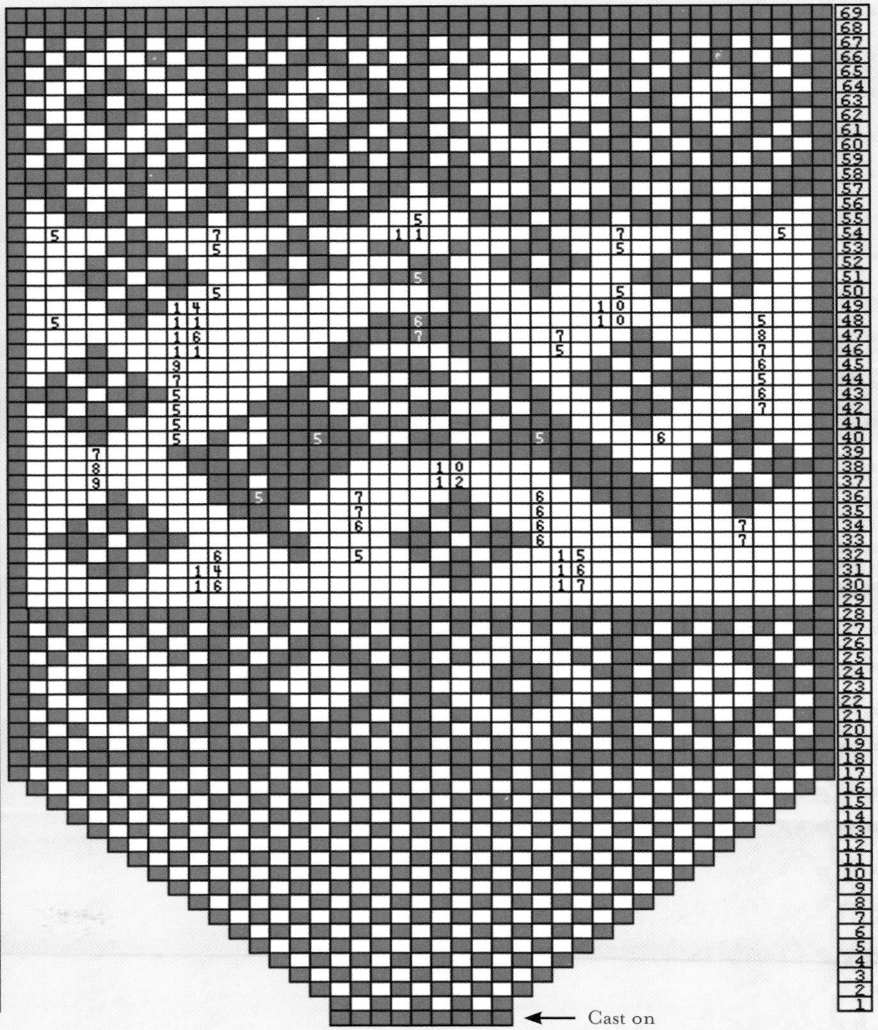

ROSES BODY

Cardinal Mittens: Use for Palm.
Sanquhar Mittens: Use for Palm and Back of Hand.

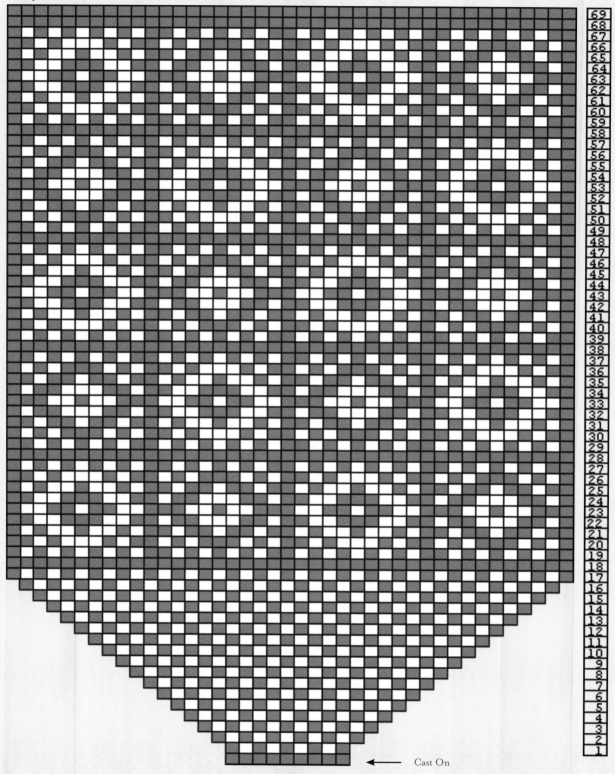

← Cast On

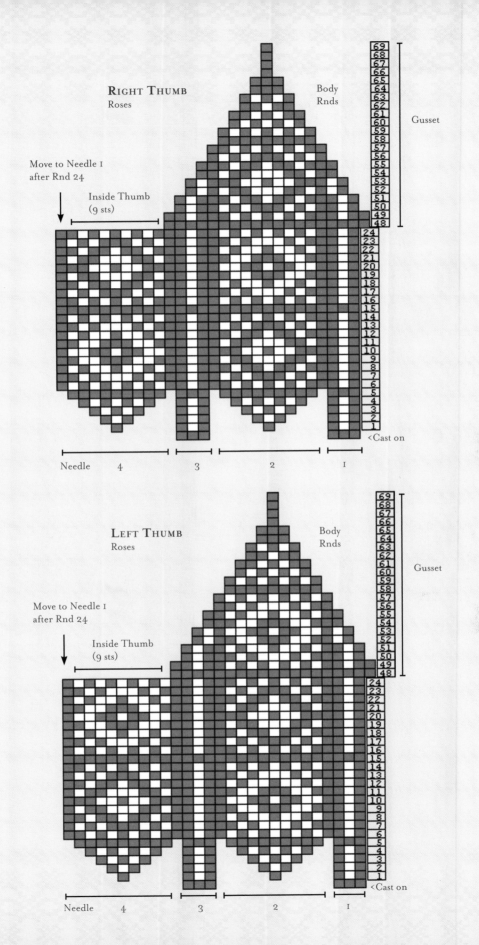

RIGHT THUMB
Roses

Body
Rnds

Gusset

Move to Needle 1
after Rnd 24

Inside Thumb
(9 sts)

Needle 4 3 2 1

<Cast on

LEFT THUMB
Roses

Body
Rnds

Gusset

Move to Needle 1
after Rnd 24

Inside Thumb
(9 sts)

Needle 4 3 2 1

<Cast on

CHICKADEE MITTENS

YARN

〰〰〰〰〰〰〰〰

I skein each of Alpaca Yarn Company Classic Lite (100% alpaca, 1.75oz/50g, 182yd/166m) in Black (MC) and White (CC)

Note: In the mitten charts, the darker color is MC and the lighter color is CC.

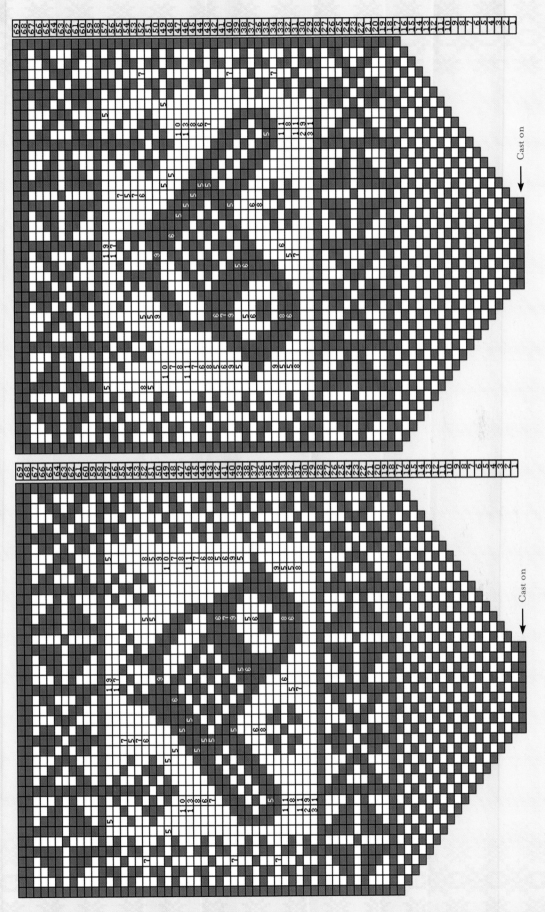

Left Chickadee Body

Right Chickadee Body

Cast on

Cast on

FLOWER AND BUTTERFLY BODY
Chickadee Mittens: Use for Palm.
Sanquhar Mittens: Use for Palm and Back of Hand.

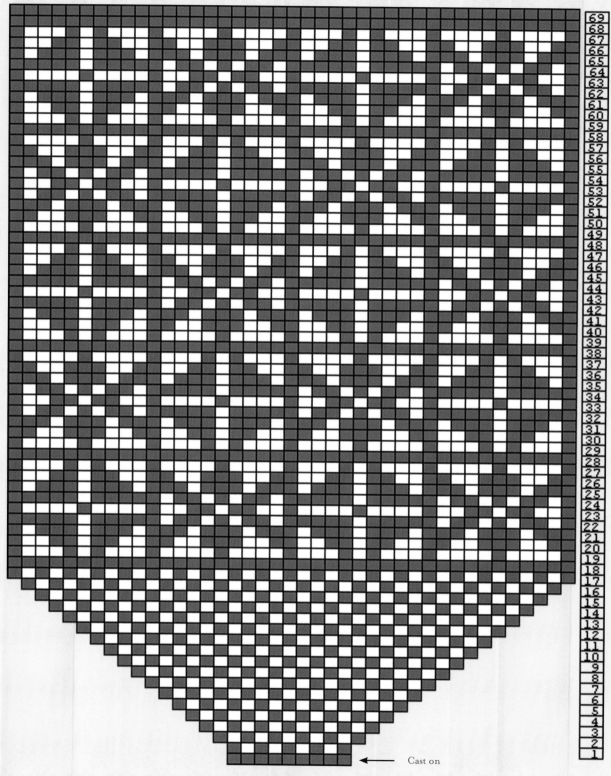

Cast on

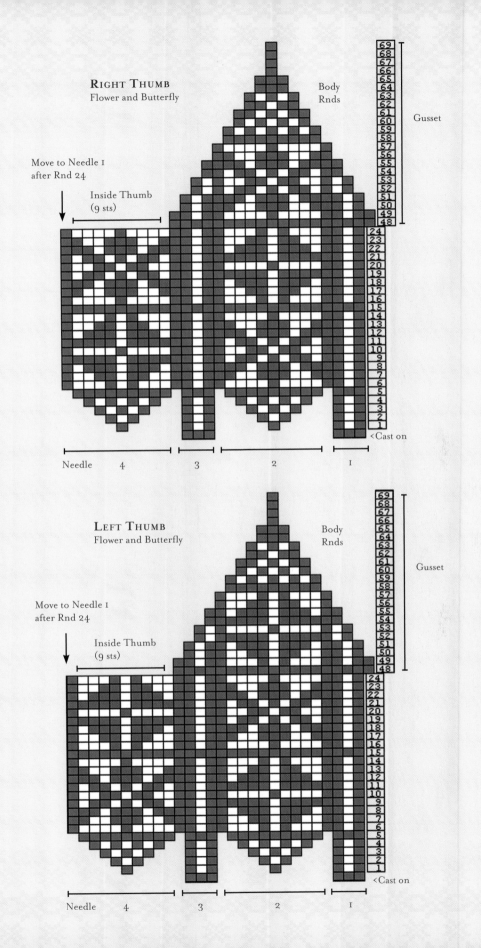

RIGHT THUMB
Flower and Butterfly

Body
Rnds

Gusset

Move to Needle 1
after Rnd 24

Inside Thumb
(9 sts)

<Cast on

Needle   4   3   2   1

LEFT THUMB
Flower and Butterfly

Body
Rnds

Gusset

Move to Needle 1
after Rnd 24

Inside Thumb
(9 sts)

<Cast on

Needle   4   3   2   1

CINNAMON TEAL MITTENS

YARN

1 skein Knit Picks Stroll Kettle
Dyed Sock (wool/nylon blend,
1.75oz/50g, 231/210m) in Auburn

1 skein Knit Picks Bare Merino,
Nylon, Donegal Sock (wool/nylon/
Donegal blend, 3.5oz/100g,
462yd/420m) in Natural (CC)

*Note: In the mitten charts, the darker
color is MC and the lighter color is CC.*

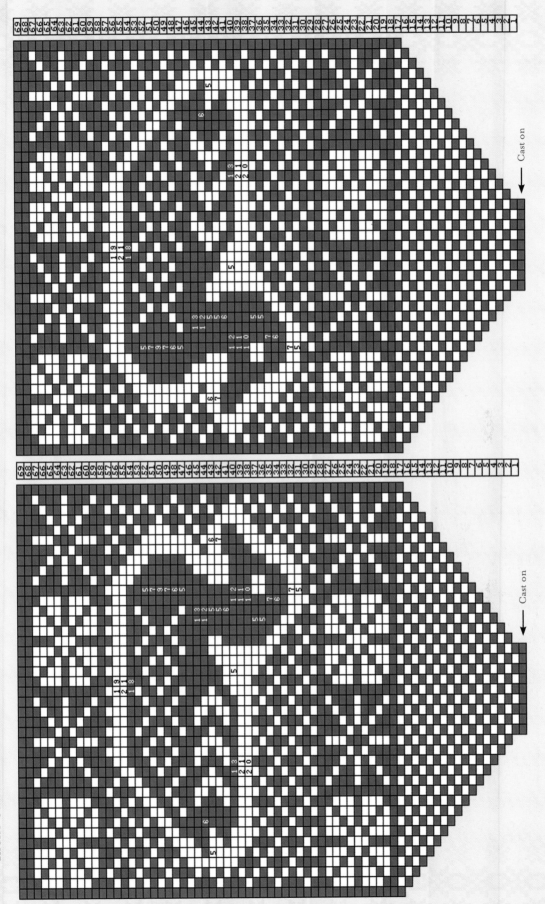

LEFT CINNAMON TEAL BODY

RIGHT CINNAMON TEAL BODY

Cast on

Cast on

Peruvian Cross Body

Cinnamon Teal Mittens: Use for Palm.
Sanquhar Mittens: Use for Palm and Back of Hand.

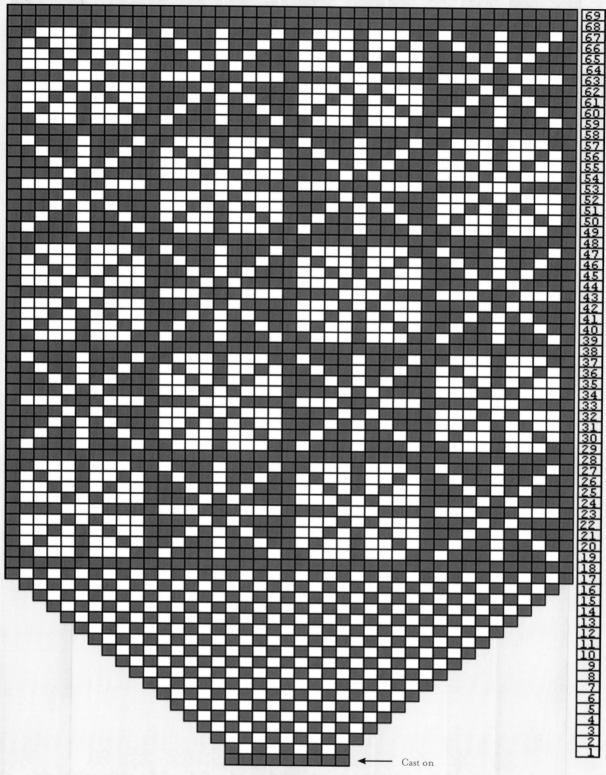

Cast on

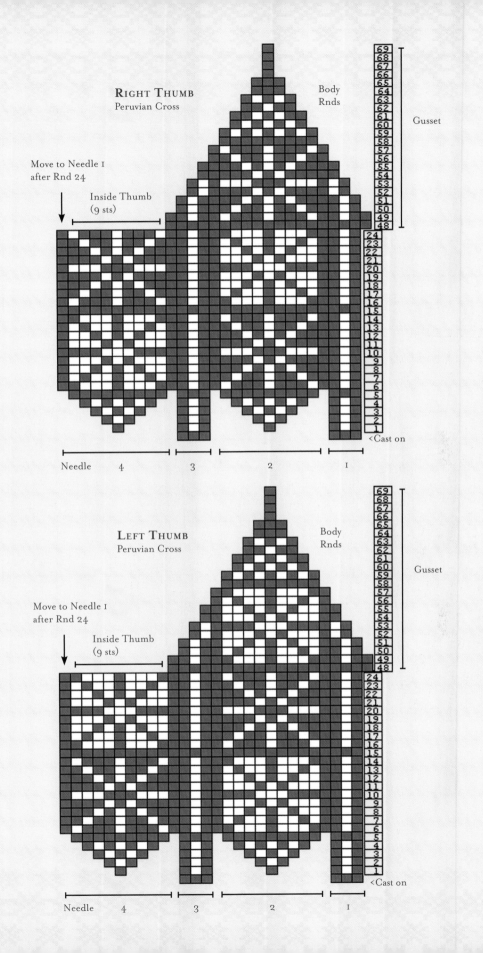

RIGHT THUMB
Peruvian Cross

Body
Rnds

Move to Needle 1
after Rnd 24

Inside Thumb
(9 sts)

Gusset

Needle   4   3   2   1

<Cast on

LEFT THUMB
Peruvian Cross

Body
Rnds

Move to Needle 1
after Rnd 24

Inside Thumb
(9 sts)

Gusset

Needle   4   3   2   1

<Cast on

GRIFFIN MITTENS

YARN

1 skein Knit Picks Stroll Multi Sock (wool/nylon blend, 1.75oz/50g, 231yd/210m) in Peacock (MC)

1 skein Knit Picks Bare Merino Wool Sock (100% wool, 3.5oz/100g, 440yd/400m) in Natural (CC)

Note: In the mitten charts, the darker color is MC and the lighter color is CC.

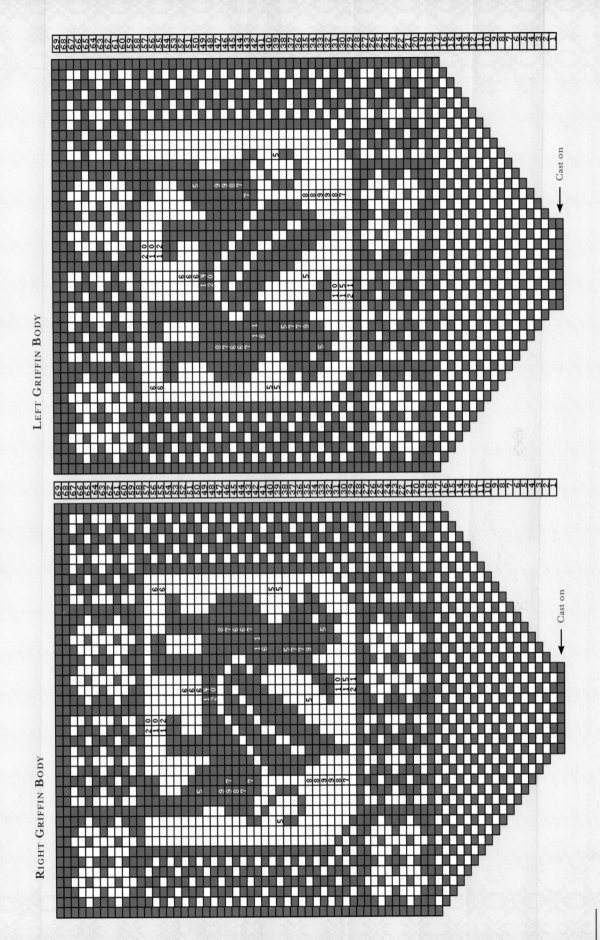

LEFT GRIFFIN BODY

RIGHT GRIFFIN BODY

Mosaic Tile Body

Griffin Mittens: Use for Palm.
Sanquhar Mittens: Use for Palm and Back of Hand.

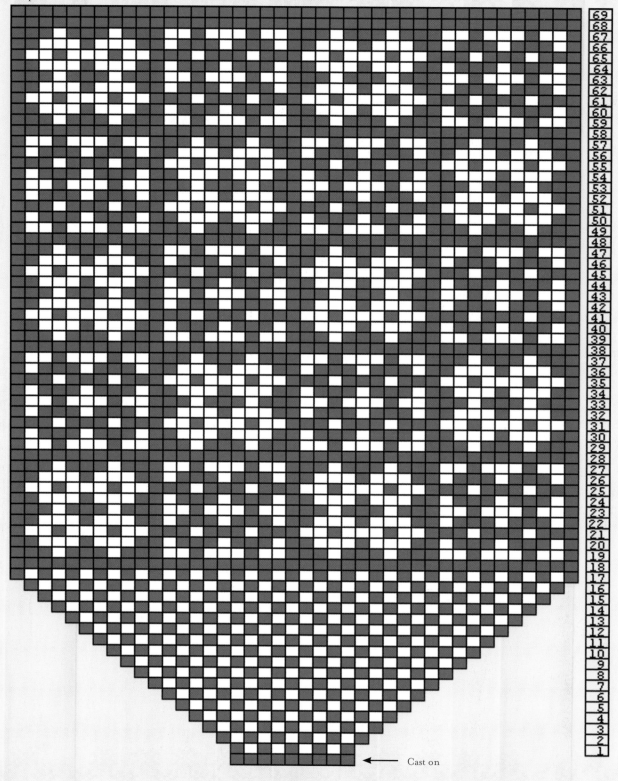

Cast on

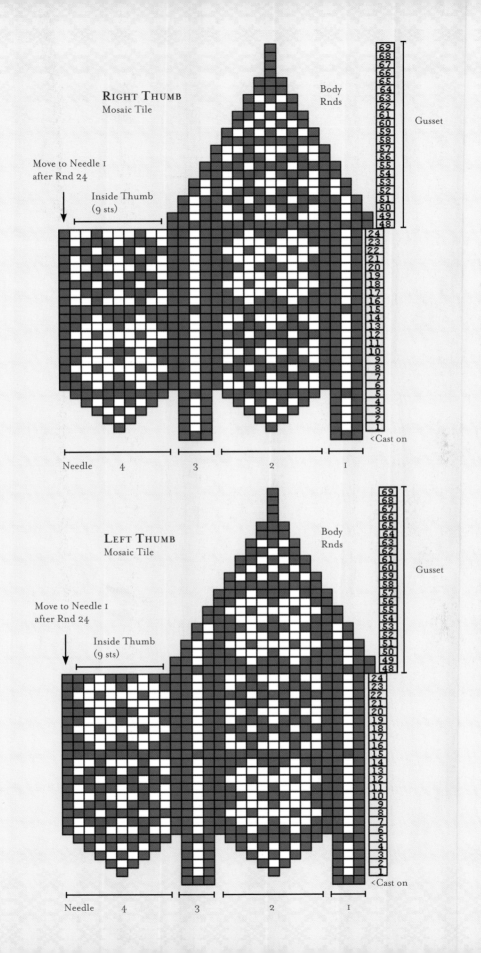

RIGHT THUMB
Mosaic Tile

Body
Rnds

Gusset

Move to Needle 1
after Rnd 24

Inside Thumb
(9 sts)

Needle   4   3   2   1

LEFT THUMB
Mosaic Tile

Body
Rnds

Gusset

Move to Needle 1
after Rnd 24

Inside Thumb
(9 sts)

Needle   4   3   2   1

GROSBEAK MITTENS

YARN

1 skein Cascade Heritage Paints
(wool/nylon blend, 3.5oz/100g,
437yd/398m) in color 9928 (MC)

1 skein Knit Picks Bare Superwash
Merino, Nylon, Donegal Sock
(wool/nylon/Donegal blend,
3.5oz/100g, 462yd/420m) in
Natural (CC)

*Note: In the mitten charts, the darker
color is MC and the lighter color is CC.*

Cast on →

Cast on →

DUKE BODY

Grosbeak Mittens: Use for Palm.
Sanquhar Mittens: Use for Palm and Back of Hand.

← Cast on

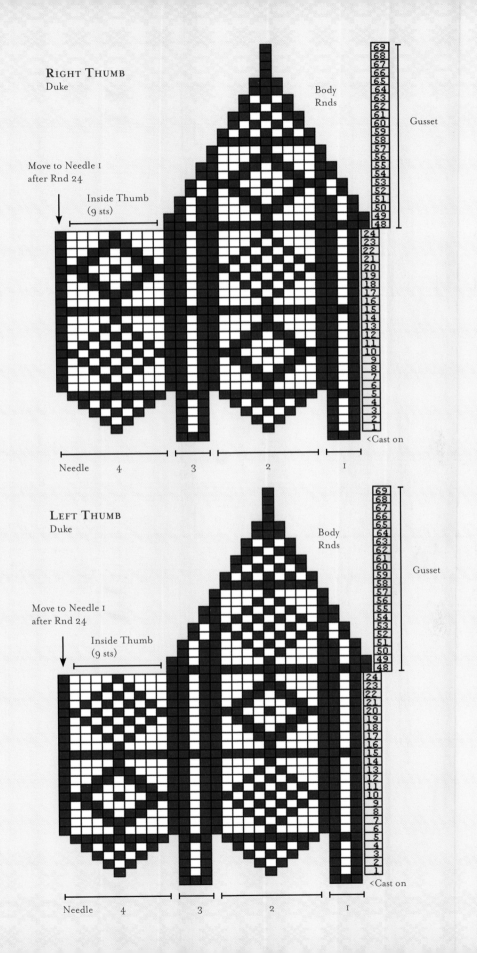

RIGHT THUMB
Duke

Body
Rnds

Gusset

Move to Needle 1
after Rnd 24

Inside Thumb
(9 sts)

<Cast on

Needle   4   3   2   1

LEFT THUMB
Duke

Body
Rnds

Gusset

Move to Needle 1
after Rnd 24

Inside Thumb
(9 sts)

<Cast on

Needle   4   3   2   1

NUTHATCH MITTENS

YARN

1 skein Alpaca Yarn Company Classic Lite (100% alpaca, 1.75oz/50g, 182yd/166m) in Gray Flannel (MC)

1 skein Knit Picks Bare Superwash Merino, Nylon, Donegal Sock (wool/nylon/Donegal blend, 3.5oz/100g, 462yd/420m) in Natural (CC)

Note: In the mitten charts, the darker color is MC and the lighter color is CC.

Left Nuthatch Body

Right Nuthatch Body

Cast on

Star and Tree Body

Nuthatch Mittens: Use for Palm.
Sanquhar Mittens: Use for Palm and Back of Hand.

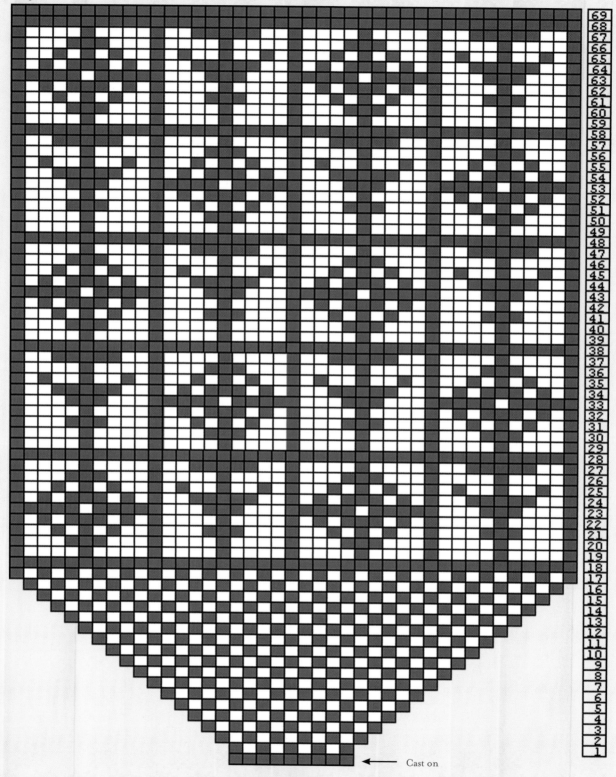

← Cast on

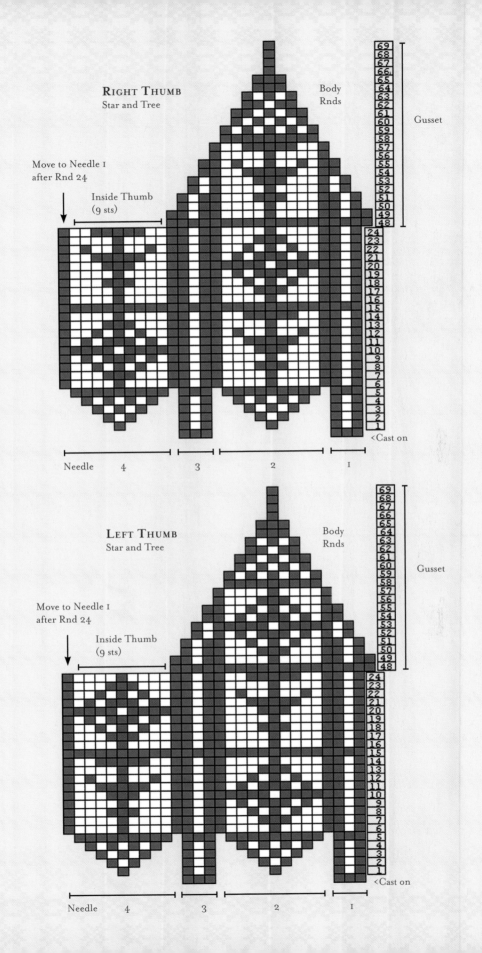

RIGHT THUMB
Star and Tree

Body
Rnds

Gusset

Move to Needle 1
after Rnd 24

Inside Thumb
(9 sts)

Needle   4   3   2   1

<Cast on

LEFT THUMB
Star and Tree

Body
Rnds

Gusset

Move to Needle 1
after Rnd 24

Inside Thumb
(9 sts)

Needle   4   3   2   1

<Cast on

REINDEER MITTENS

YARN

1 skein Alpaca Yarn Company Classic Lite (100% alpaca, 1.75oz/50g, 182yd/166m) in Patriot Red (MC)

1 skein Knit Picks Bare Superwash Merino, Nylon, Donegal Sock (wool/nylon/Donegal blend, 3.5oz/100g, 462yd/420m) in Natural (CC)

Note: In the mitten charts, the darker color is MC and the lighter color is CC.

LEFT REINDEER BODY

Cast on

RIGHT REINDEER BODY

Cast on

STAR AND SNOWFLAKE BODY

Reindeer Mittens: Use for Palm.
Sanquhar Mittens: Use for Palm and Back of Hand.

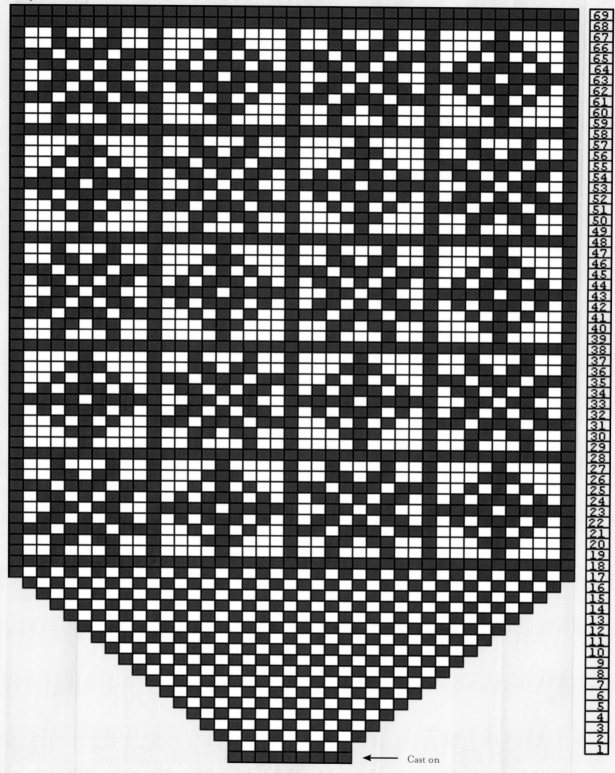

← Cast on

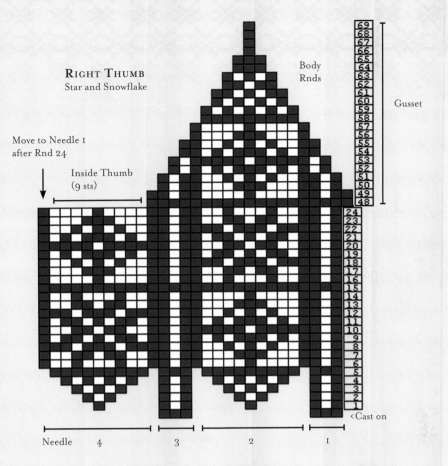

RIGHT THUMB
Star and Snowflake

Move to Needle 1
after Rnd 24

Inside Thumb
(9 sts)

Body
Rnds

Gusset

Needle   4   3   2   1

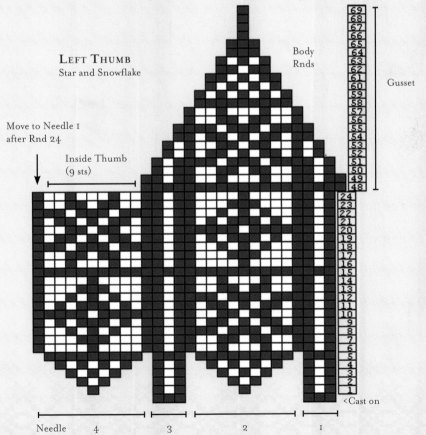

LEFT THUMB
Star and Snowflake

Move to Needle 1
after Rnd 24

Inside Thumb
(9 sts)

Body
Rnds

Gusset

Needle   4   3   2   1

WOOD DUCK MITTENS

YARN

1 skein Dragonfly Fibers Dragon Sock (100% wool, 4oz/113g, 400yd/364m) in Gaugin's Polynesia (MC)

1 skein Knit Picks Bare Peruvian Highland Wool Fingering (100% wool, 3.5oz/100g, 440yd/400m) in Natural (CC)

Note: In the mitten charts, the darker color is MC and the lighter color is CC.

Cast on →

Cast on →

Sun and Walnut Body

Wood Duck Mittens: Use for Palm.
Sanquhar Mittens: Use for Palm and Back of Hand.

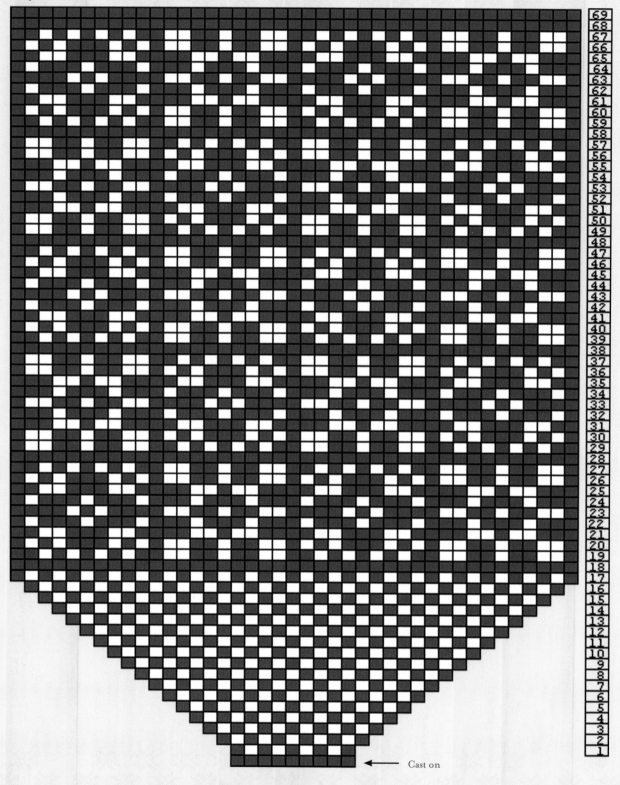

← Cast on

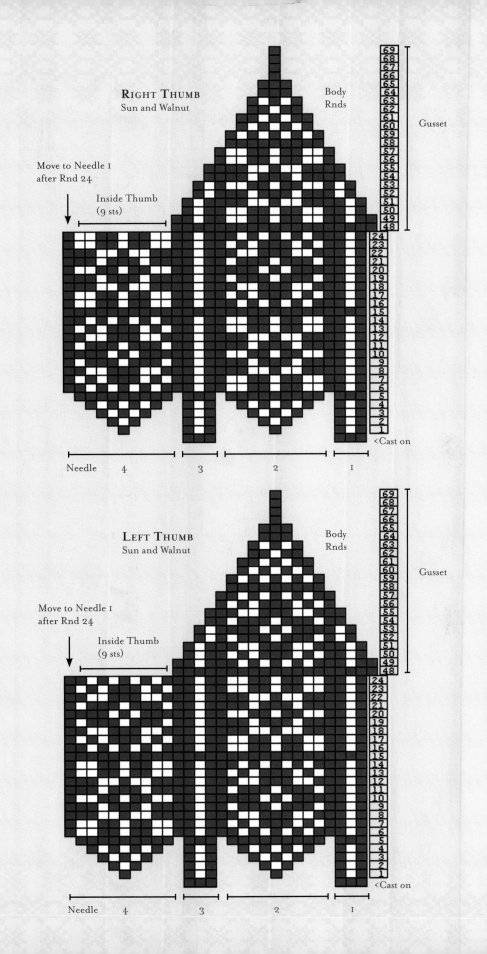

RIGHT THUMB
Sun and Walnut

Body
Rnds

Gusset

Move to Needle 1
after Rnd 24

Inside Thumb
(9 sts)

<Cast on

Needle   4   3   2   I

LEFT THUMB
Sun and Walnut

Body
Rnds

Gusset

Move to Needle 1
after Rnd 24

Inside Thumb
(9 sts)

<Cast on

Needle   4   3   2   I

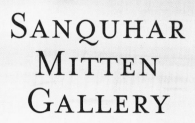

SANQUHAR
MITTEN
GALLERY

GLOVES

I've always loved looking at photographs of Sanquhar and Fair Isle gloves in knitting books or magazines. I was convinced that I would never knit a pair of these intricate beauties. I hated making the thumbs on mittens, and knitting gloves made me cringe because, in addition to the thumb, I'd have to deal with the four fingers. Imagine knitting the few stitches used for the thumb with the weight of the mitten body working against you. Now multiply that vision by five and you have the nightmare I associated with glove making.

My attitude changed a decade ago when I knit my first pair of finger-to-cuff gloves. I began with simple worsted weight gloves and gradually added patterns to the glove body and then the fingers. To ensure that the fingers were joined in the correct order, I created a foamcore template of my hand with open fingers. I stored the finished fingers and thumb on this template until I was ready to join the pieces. I still recommend this technique to beginning glove makers because it lets you check the finger patterns to ensure that the glove palms all lie on one side of the template and the glove backs lie on the opposite side. Once the fingers are joined together, correcting any misalignment is more difficult. A template also lets me create a glove with a custom fit.

I have designed finger-to-cuff gloves using a variety of knitting techniques, including Sanquhar, Fair Isle and knotwork, and knit dozens of pairs in each technique. I love making gloves, and I think that you will share my joy once you've mastered the finger-to-cuff technique.

FLIP-TOP MITTENS

Several years ago, my father requested mittens he could use while working around his log cabin in the Wisconsin woods. His requirements included glove fingers that ended before the first knuckle, a full thumb and a mitten hood that pulled over the fingers. To create these beauties, I needed two templates of Dad's hand: one with open fingers to design the glove portion and a second with closed fingers to design the mitten portion. Necessity being the mother of invention, Dad used corrugated cardboard cut with his jigsaw to create my models. These first mittens were simple, but toasty warm. The designs featured here use salt-and-pepper fingers, a bird or beast hood and a Sanquhar design of your choice for the body. I've given away many flip-top mittens as gifts. They're fun to knit and useful for a variety of winter tasks including driving, snow shoveling and dog walking.

BASIC GLOVE PATTERN

A finger-to-cuff glove begins with the thumb, which is knit first and placed on safety pins until needed. Next, knit the fingers beginning with the little finger, followed by the ring, middle and finally the index finger. The little, ring and middle fingers are placed on safety pins until needed for the body. Storing the finished fingers on a foamcore glove template ensures that the fingers are kept in the correct order.

The fingers and thumbs begin with the salt-and-pepper pattern containing the increases. The Sanquhar finger or thumb pattern is knit next. Repeat this pattern twice for the thumb and all fingers except the little finger which uses only one repeat. Once completed, join the fingers to construct the glove body.

If making a bird or beast glove, follow the bird or beast design for the back of the hand; otherwise, use the desired Sanquhar glove body pattern. Use the Sanquhar body pattern for the palm of the gloves. After two repetitions of the Sanquhar body pattern, attach the thumb to the glove body using a 3-Needle bind off, which secures the inner palm and inner thumb stitches. If knitting a bird or beast glove, continue to follow the bird or beast design for the back of the hand and the Sanquhar body pattern for the palm.

Salt-and-pepper rounds are worked upon completion of the pattern charts. Typically, seven rounds are required to reach the wrist, but you may add or subtract salt-and-pepper rounds for the correct length. A final round knit in MC (dark yarn) precedes the ribbing. The glove ends with 20 rounds of corrugated knitting.

SIZE

One size fits most women

NEEDLES

One set of 6" (15cm) US 0 (2mm) double-pointed needles

One set of 8" (20cm) US 0 (2mm) double-pointed needles

If necessary, change needle size to obtain correct gauge.

GAUGE

42 sts and 40 rows = 4" (10cm) in St st

CUSTOMIZING THE GLOVES

The finished gloves should fit most women; however, the designs lend themselves well to modification. When I began my designs, I created a foamcore template of the recipient's hand. I knit the thumb, adjusting the number of salt-and-pepper rounds until the thumb barely touched the bottom of the thumb on the foamcore model. Similarly, I constructed the fingers by adjusting the salt-and-pepper rounds until each finger reached the edge of the palm.

Unless you're creating gloves for someone with abnormally small or large hands, you should not need to adjust the width of the patterns.

GLOVES

THUMB

Note: Each patt has its own left and right thumb chart. Refer to that chart when knitting the thumbs.

Cast on 6 sts and distribute evenly onto 2 needles, using Turkish cast on and MC. Knit across the sts on each needle.

Note: Refer to the thumb chart for the desired Sanquhar patt. Because the first rnd contains a single inc, it is easier to combine Needles 1 and 2 onto the first needle and Needles 3 and 4 onto the second needle. This lessens the possibility of the sts slipping off the ends of the needles.

Thumb Rnd 1 (inc rnd):

First Needle: K3 following Sanquhar thumb chart for Needle 1. M1 following Sanquhar thumb chart for Needle 2.

Second Needle: K3 following Sanquhar thumb chart for Needle 3. M1 following Sanquhar thumb chart for Needle 4—8 sts.

Thumb Rnd 2 (inc rnd):

Needle 1: K3 following Sanquhar thumb chart for Needle 1—1 st rem on LH needle.

Needle 2: With a new needle (Needle 2), incR using MC. Knit next st using CC. IncL using MC.

Needle 3: K3 following Sanquhar thumb chart for Needle 3—1 st rem on LH needle.

Needle 4: IncR using MC. Knit the next st using CC. IncL using MC—12 sts.

Thumb Rnds 3–6 (inc rnds):

Cont to foll Sanquhar thumb chart for desired thumb (right or left), increasing 1 st at each end of Needle 2 and Needle 4 as shown on chart—28 sts after Rnd 6.

Note: Rnd 3 and 4 increases are in the salt-and-pepper patt while Rnd 5 and 6 increases are in the Sanquhar patt.

Thumb Rnds 7–23: Foll Sanquhar thumb chart for desired thumb (right or left).

Thumb Rnd 24: Knit to last st of rnd following Sanquhar thumb chart. Place last st of Needle 4 onto Needle 1. Place first st of Needle 4 onto Needle 3. Purl across rem 9 sts on Needle 4 using MC. Place these 9 inside thumb sts on a safety pin. Divide the 19 rem sts between 2 safety pins. Cut yarns, leaving long tails. Set the thumb aside until you reach Rnd 48 of the glove body.

GLOVE FINGERS

Note: Make the index finger last, and do not cut the yarn.

With the 6" (15cm) dpns, cast on 6 sts and distribute evenly onto 2 needles, using Turkish cast on and MC. Knit across the sts on each needle.

Finger Rnd 1 (inc rnd):

First Needle: K3 following Sanquhar finger chart for Needle 1. M1 in CC.

Second Needle: K3 following Sanquhar finger chart for Needle 2. M1 in CC—8 sts.

Finger Rnd 2 (inc rnd):

Needle 1: K3 in MC following Sanquhar finger chart—1 st rem on LH needle.

Needle 2: With a new needle (Needle 2), incR using CC. Knit the next st using MC. IncL using CC.

Needle 3: K3 in MC—1 st rem on LH needle.

Needle 4: IncR using CC. Knit the next st using MC. IncL using CC—12 sts.

Finger Rnds 3–5 (inc rnds):

Cont to foll the Sanquhar finger chart for the desired finger, increasing 1 st at each end of Needle 2 and Needle 4 as shown on chart—24 sts after Rnd 5.

Salt-and-Pepper Rnds: Complete the number of salt-and-pepper rnds for the desired finger as indicated in the Sanquhar finger chart.

Sanquhar Finger Rnds: After you have completed the salt-and-pepper rnds, foll Sanquhar finger chart for each finger. Notice that the middle finger begins with Needle 3, and the little finger ends after Rnd 10.

Cut the yarns, leaving long tails. Secure the live sts of each finger on 4 safety pins, dividing the sts as such: 2, 10, 2, 10.

For the index finger, knit this finger after the other fingers and the thumb. Do not cut the yarn.

CONNECTING FINGERS

Once all the fingers and the thumb have been knit for one glove, assemble the glove body. Beginning with the little finger, remove the 2 between-finger sts from the little finger and place them on a 6" (15cm) needle. (The between-finger sts for the little finger are those next to the cut yarn.) Remove the 2 between-finger sts from the ring finger (the 2 sts opposite the cut yarn). Place these sts on a second 6" (15cm) needle.

Place the right sides of the little and ring fingers together. Make sure that the Sanquhar patterns alternate. With a yarn tail from the little finger, use the 3-Needle bind off to secure the 2 fingers, but do not cut the yarn when you are finished.

Rep this procedure to join the ring finger to the middle finger and the middle finger to the index finger.

Remove 12 index finger sts from the safety pins and place on an 8" (20cm) double-pointed needle. (These will be the 2 sts next to the live yarns and the 10 index finger sts to the left of the 2 live sts.)

Remove the adjacent 10 middle finger sts and the adjacent ring finger sts and place them on the needle. Remove the adjacent 10 little finger sts and add them to the needle.

Remove the rem 12 little finger sts from the safety pins and place them on a second needle. (This will be the 2 rem little finger sts and the 10 little finger sts adjacent to them.) Remove the 10 rem ring finger sts and place them on the second needle.

Remove the 10 rem middle finger sts and place them on a third needle. Remove the 10 rem index finger sts and place them on the third needle. You should have a total of 84 sts (42 on the palm and 42 on the back of the hand).

GLOVE BODY

The glove body uses the bird or beast body chart for the back of the hand and the Sanquhar body chart for the palm.

Rnd 1: Using MC, sl 1, k2tog, psso, k39, sl 1, k2tog, psso, k39—80 sts. (This replaces Rnd 1 of Sanquhar body chart and bird or beast body chart.)

Rnds 2–20:

RIGHT GLOVE: Foll bird or beast body chart for the first 40 sts and Sanquhar body chart for the last 40 sts.

LEFT GLOVE: Foll Sanquhar body chart for the first 40 sts and bird or beast body chart for the last 40 sts.

ATTACH THUMB

Rnd 21:

Note: The thumb gusset replaces the last Sanquhar box on the right mitten and the first Sanquhar box on the left mitten. No additional sts are cast on for the thumb.

RIGHT GLOVE: Knit back of hand using bird or beast body chart. Knit palm using Sanquhar body chart, working only 30 sts (3 Sanquhar boxes)—10 sts (1 Sanquhar box) rem on needle. Remove inside thumb sts from the holder and place on a needle. Use 3-Needle bind off to bind off the next 9 palm sts with the 9 inside thumb sts. Place rem thumb sts onto the needle. Knit these sts using the right thumb gusset chart. Knit the last st in MC.

LEFT GLOVE: Remove the 9 inside thumb sts from holder and place on a needle. Knit the first st in MC, then use 3-Needle bind off to bind off the next 9 palm sts with the 9 inside thumb sts. Place rem thumb sts on the needle. Knit these sts using the left thumb gusset chart. Knit the palm sts using the Sanquhar body chart. Knit the back of the hand using the bird or beast body chart.

Rnd 22:

RIGHT GLOVE: Foll bird or beast body chart, Sanquhar body chart and right thumb gusset chart.

LEFT GLOVE: Foll left thumb gusset chart, Sanquhar body chart and bird or beast body chart.

Rnds 23–31: Cont to foll the Sanquhar body and thumb gusset charts and the bird or beast body chart as directed for the left and right gloves.

AT THE SAME TIME:

Rnd 25: Work Sanquhar thumb gusset dec as k1, sl 1, k1 (CC), psso. Work in patt to last 3 sts, k2tog (CC), k1. This maintains the white border stripe for 5 rnds. Cont to foll Sanquhar body and thumb gusset charts and the bird or beast body chart as directed for the right and left gloves.

Salt-and-Pepper Rnds: Foll salt-and-pepper patt for 7 rnds. On the first salt-and-pepper rnd, decreasing 6 sts evenly across the rnd—74 sts.

Knit 1 rnd in MC.

CUFF

Work 20 rnds of corrugated ribbing (k2 MC, p2 CC), decreasing 6 sts evenly across the first rnd—68 sts.

Bind off in MC. Weave in all ends and block.

SALT-AND-PEPPER PATTERN

Rnd 1 and all odd rnds: *Knit 1 CC, knit 1 MC; rep from * around.

Rnd 2 and all even rnds: *Knit 1 MC, knit 1 CC; rep from * around.

Sanquhar Gloves

I have always been fascinated with Sanquhar gloves; I love the little boxes. Although I use white as the contrasting color for the bird or beast versions, any light-color yarn works well with the Sanquhar-only versions. To make gloves with only the Sanquhar design, simply knit the glove body pattern for both the palm and back of the hand.

Bird or Beast Gloves Using a Different Sanquhar Pattern

To make bird or beast gloves with a different Sanquhar pattern, follow the thumb and finger directions for the Sanquhar pattern of your choice. Follow the directions for the bird or beast gloves, substituting your desired Sanquhar pattern for the palm.

Fingerless Gloves

I have given away many pairs of these gloves as gifts. Because the fingers and thumbs are open, the gloves come in handy when you need finger dexterity. They are useful for dog training, driving or working in a cold room.

THUMBS

Note: You may use either a two-color long tail or braided long tail cast on for the fingerless glove fingers and thumbs (see Knitting Glossary, page 155).

Using the 6" (15cm) dpns, cast on 28 sts with 9 sts each on Needles 1 and 3 and 10 sts on Needle 2.

Work 3 rnds of Latvian Braid (see next page).

Work 8 rnds in the salt-and-pepper patt (see page 105). After the last rnd, purl across the 9 sts on Needle 3 using MC. Place these 9 sts on a safety pin for the inner thumb. Divide the rem 19 sts between 2 safety pins. Cut the yarns, leaving long tails.

FINGERS

Using the 6" (15cm) dpns, cast 24 sts onto 3 needles so that each needle has 8 sts.

Work 3 rnds of Latvian Braid.

Salt-and-Pepper Rnds: Work salt-and-pepper patt for the indicated number of rnds for each finger.

Little Finger: 6 rnds.

Ring Finger: 8 rnds.

Middle Finger: 10 rnds.

Index Finger: 7 rnds (DO NOT CUT THE YARN).

Cut the yarns on all fingers except index finger, leaving long tails. Place the sts on each of 4 safety pins divided as follows: 2, 10, 2, 10.

FINGERLESS GLOVE BODY

Foll the bird or beast glove instructions on pages 104–105 for joining the fingers to create a glove body and knitting the glove bodies.

Latvian Braid Pattern

Rnd 1: K1 with MC, k1 with CC.

Rnd 2: Bring both yarns to the front. P1 with MC. Bring CC over MC and p1 with CC. Bring the MC over CC and p1 with MC. Cont to end of rnd.

Rnd 3: Bring MC under CC and p1 with MC. Bring CC under MC and p1 with CC. Cont to end of rnd.

Note: After knitting the Latvian braid, bring the cast-on yarn tails up through the inside of the finger or thumb. Loop them over the knitting yarns as you would for a yarn carry. Continue to loop them over the yarns every second st for 16 sts. After you finish the finger or thumb, clip the yarn ends. This secures the yarn ends so that no amount of tugging will loosen them.

Glove Hints

- The initial three rounds of the fingers and thumbs are difficult because you have only a few stitches on each needle. Once you make it past these rounds, the knitting becomes easier.
- After Round 10 of the fingers or thumbs you might wish to weave the cast-on yarn tail to the inside of the finger or thumb. This not only gets the yarn tails out of your way, but it saves you time later.
- The stitches will be stiff on the first two or three rounds because you're changing the shape of the knitting. Don't worry; they loosen up.
- Although the Sanquhar pattern charts show four needles in action, I typically only use three for ease in knitting. Feel free to divide the stitches as you see fit.

Minimizing Holes Between Fingers and Thumbs

You will notice a gap where each finger meets its neighbor and, when you attach the thumb, where the thumb joins the mitten body. Slip the stitch before the gap. Pick up the left and right stitches from the round below the gap. Knit these two stitches together. Pass the slipped stitch over the stitches knit together. (Essentially, this is a sl 1, k2tog, psso.) Do this for each side of the finger or thumb. Any remaining gap will be very small, and you can use the tails remaining from the 3-Needle bind off to close them.

Basic Flip-Top Mitten Pattern

Flip-top mittens feature a mitten hood which is knit first and stored on a spare needle until it is ready to be attached to its half-finger glove body. The hood begins with a Turkish cast on, leaving long yarn tails to make the button clasp. The back of the hood features a bird or beast design, while the palm side begins with the salt-and-pepper pattern and ends with two repetitions of a Sanquhar pattern. Although I chose Sanquhar patterns for the featured flip-tops, you may use any pattern that you wish. The only requirement is that you begin your palm pattern from the second Sanquhar body repeat (Round 11). This ensures the correct alignment of the hood and body patterns.

All hoods except the butterfly use separate charts for the left and right bird or beast. As was true of the mittens, the left hood contains a right-facing bird or beast while the right hood contains a left-facing bird or beast.

The hood instructions give two options for ending the hood: a picot edge or a ribbed edge. After completing the hood, knit the Sanquhar thumb chart and store it on safety pins as directed in the glove instructions. Next, the half-finger glove fingers are knit, beginning with the little finger and ending with the index finger. Once finished, the fingers are joined to create the body. On the twelfth round, the hood is attached. Placement of the hood varies depending on which flip-top you are knitting. For the right flip-top, the hood is joined to the body on the last 40 stitches and wraps to the first stitch of the next round. For the left flip-top, the hood is joined with the body on the first 41 stitches.

On the twenty-first round, the thumb is joined to the body. Salt-and-pepper rounds end the body, followed by one round knit in the main color only and twenty rounds of corrugated ribbing. Buttons added to the palm side of each flip-top are the finishing touch.

SIZE

One size fits most women

NEEDLES

One set of 8" (20cm) size 0 (2mm) double-pointed needles

One set of 6" (15cm) size 0 (2mm) double-pointed needles

If necessary, change needle size to obtain correct gauge.

OTHER

Two ½" (1cm) or ⅝" (16mm) buttons

GAUGE

42 sts and 40 rows = 4" (10cm) in St st

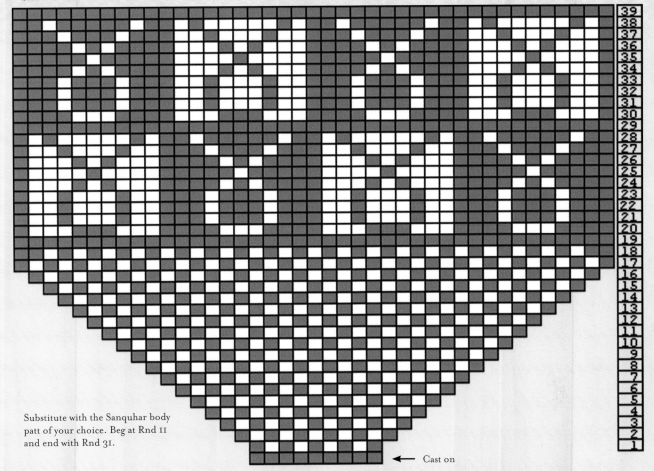

39
38
37
36
35
34
33
32
31
30
29
28
27
26
25
24
23
22
21
20
19
18
17
16
15
14
13
12
11
10
9
8
7
6
5
4
3
2
1

Substitute with the Sanquhar body
patt of your choice. Beg at Rnd 11
and end with Rnd 31.

← Cast on

FLIP-TOP MITTENS

HOOD

Cast on 18 sts and distribute evenly on 2 needles, using Turkish cast on and the 6" (15cm) needles. Leave long yarn tails for creating the button clasp. Knit across the sts on each needle.

Rnd 1: Foll bird or beast hood chart for the back of the hand. Work salt-and-pepper hood chart as illustrated on page 107 for the palm.

Rnds 2–17 (inc rnds): Foll bird or beast hood chart for the back of the hand and salt-and-pepper hood chart for the palm. IncR after first st and incL before last st on each side of the back of the hand and the palm of the hand.

Rnd 18: Foll bird or beast hood chart for the back of the hand and salt-and-pepper hood chart for the palm.

Rnds 19–39: Cont to foll hood chart for the back of the hand. For the palm, knit Rnds 11–31 of the Sanquhar patt of your choice.

Cut CC, leaving a long tail. Place the 41 palm sts onto a holder or a piece of scrap yarn until needed. Finish the bird or beast side of the hood with either the Ribbed or Picot Edge (see right).

BUTTON CLASP

Because CC yarn starts at a different point, weave it into place on the inside of the hood until it is in the same place as the MC yarn. Pull both starting yarns through to the outside of the hood at the second st. Knit the yarns and the second st on the outside tog. Knit the yarns on the needle 5 more times (to form a chain). Knit the yarns and the eighth st on the hood crown tog. Pull the yarns through the st to secure (like the last st in a bind off). Bring the yarns to the inside and anchor them firmly. Weave in the yarn tails.

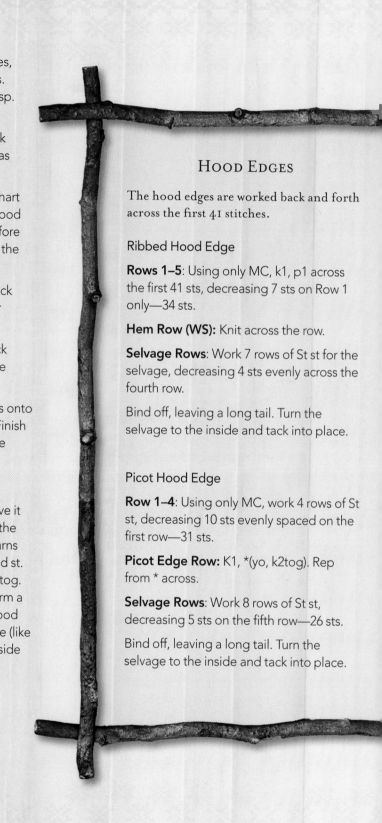

HOOD EDGES

The hood edges are worked back and forth across the first 41 stitches.

Ribbed Hood Edge

Rows 1–5: Using only MC, k1, p1 across the first 41 sts, decreasing 7 sts on Row 1 only—34 sts.

Hem Row (WS): Knit across the row.

Selvage Rows: Work 7 rows of St st for the selvage, decreasing 4 sts evenly across the fourth row.

Bind off, leaving a long tail. Turn the selvage to the inside and tack into place.

Picot Hood Edge

Row 1–4: Using only MC, work 4 rows of St st, decreasing 10 sts evenly spaced on the first row—31 sts.

Picot Edge Row: K1, *(yo, k2tog). Rep from * across.

Selvage Rows: Work 8 rows of St st, decreasing 5 sts on the fifth row—26 sts.

Bind off, leaving a long tail. Turn the selvage to the inside and tack into place.

THUMB

Note: Each patt has its own left and right thumb chart. Refer to that chart when knitting the flip-top thumbs.

Using Turkish cast on and MC, cast on 6 sts and distribute evenly onto 2 needles. Knit across the sts on each needle.

Note: Refer to the thumb chart for the desired Sanquhar patt. Because the first rnd contains a single inc, it is easier to combine Needles 1 and 2 onto the first needle and Needles 3 and 4 onto the second needle. This lessens the possibility of the sts slipping off the ends of the needles.

Thumb Rnd 1 (inc rnd):

First needle: K3 following Sanquhar thumb chart for Needle 1. M1 following Sanquhar thumb chart for Needle 2.

Second needle: K3 following Sanquhar thumb chart for Needle 3. M1 following Sanquhar thumb chart for Needle 4—8 sts.

Thumb Rnd 2 (inc rnd):

Needle 1: K3 following Sanquhar thumb chart for Needle 1—1 st rem on LH needle.

Needle 2: With a new needle (Needle 2), incR using MC. Knit the next st using CC. IncL using MC.

Needle 3: K3 following Sanquhar thumb chart for Needle 3—1 st rem on LH needle.

Needle 4: IncR using MC. Knit the next st using CC. IncL using MC—12 sts.

Thumb Rnds 3–6 (inc rnds): Cont to foll Sanquhar thumb chart for the desired thumb (right or left), increasing 1 st at each end of Needle 2 and Needle 4 as shown on the patt chart—28 sts after Rnd 6.

Note: Rnd 3 and 4 increases are in the salt-and-pepper patt, while Rnd 5 and 6 increases are in the Sanquhar patt.

Thumb Rnds 7–23: Foll Sanquhar thumb chart for the desired thumb (right or left).

Thumb Rnd 24: Knit to last st of rnd following Sanquhar thumb chart. Place the last st of Needle 4 onto Needle 1. Place the first st of Needle 4 onto Needle 3. Purl across rem 9 sts on Needle 4 using MC. Place these 9 inside thumb sts on a safety pin. Divide the 19 remaining sts between 2 safety pins. Cut the yarns, leaving long tails. Set the thumb aside until you reach Rnd 21 of the flip-top body.

FINGERS

Using the 6" (15cm) dpns, cast on 24 sts and divide evenly onto 3 needles—8 sts on each needle.

Work 3 rnds of Latvian Braid (see page 107).

Salt-and-Pepper Rnds: Work salt-and-pepper patt for the indicated number of rnds for each finger.

Little Finger: 6 rnds.

Ring Finger: 8 rnds.

Middle Finger: 10 rnds.

Index Finger: 7 rnds (DO NOT CUT THE YARN).

Cut the yarns on all fingers except index finger, leaving long tails. Secure the live sts of each finger on 4 safety pins, dividing the sts as follows: 2, 10, 2, 10.

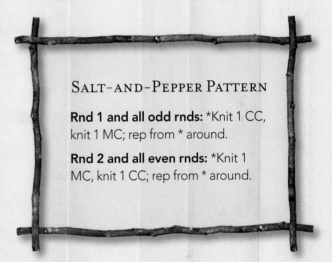

SALT-AND-PEPPER PATTERN

Rnd 1 and all odd rnds: *Knit 1 CC, knit 1 MC; rep from * around.

Rnd 2 and all even rnds: *Knit 1 MC, knit 1 CC; rep from * around.

CONNECTING FINGERS

Once all the fingers and the thumb have been knit for the flip-top, assemble the body. Beginning with the little finger, remove the 2 between-finger sts from the little finger and place on a 6" (15cm) needle. (The between-finger sts for the little finger are those next to the cut yarn.) Remove the 2 between-finger sts from the ring finger (the 2 sts opposite the cut yarn.) Place these sts on a second 6" (15cm) needle.

Place the right sides of the little and ring fingers together. Make sure that the Sanquhar patterns alternate. With a yarn tail from the little finger, use the 3-Needle bind off to secure the 2 fingers, but do not cut the yarn when you are finished.

Rep this procedure to join the ring finger to the middle finger and the middle finger to the index finger.

Remove 12 index finger sts from the safety pins and place on an 8" (20cm) double-pointed needle. (This will be the 2 sts next to the live yarns and the 10 index finger sts to the left of the 2 live sts.)

Remove the adjacent 10 middle finger sts and the adjacent ring finger sts and place them on the needle. Remove the adjacent 10 little finger sts and add them to the needle.

Remove the rem 12 little finger sts from the safety pins and place them on a second needle. (This will be the 2 rem little finger sts and the 10 little finger sts adjacent to them.) Remove the 10 rem ring finger sts and place them on the second needle.

Remove the 10 rem middle finger sts and place them on a third needle. Remove the 10 rem index finger sts and place them on the third needle. You should have a total of 84 sts (42 on the palm and 42 on the back of the hand).

FLIP-TOP BODY

Note: The flip-top bodies use only the Sanquhar body chart. You will rep 1 row of this patt 4 times for each rnd.

Rnd 1: Using MC, sl 1, k2tog, psso, k39, sl 1, k2tog, psso, k39—80 sts. (This replaces Rnd 1 of the Sanquhar body chart.)

Rnds 2–11: Foll the Sanquhar body chart.

ATTACH HOOD
Rnd 12:

RIGHT FLIP-TOP: Foll Sanquhar body chart for the first 40 sts. Remove the hood sts from the holder or scrap yarn and place them on a needle. Align the hood palm patt so it matches the Sanquhar body patt. The Sanquhar patt will be in front of you and the bird or beast design will be away from you.

Knit tog 1 st from the hood and 1 st from the palm following Sanquhar body chart.

Note: Because the hood contains 41 sts and the palm contains only 40 sts, the last hood st will be knit tog with the first back of the hand st on the next rnd.

LEFT FLIP-TOP: Place the hood over the palm as indicated for the right flip-top. For the next 41 sts, knit tog 1 st from the hood and 1 st from the palm following Sanquhar body chart.

Knit the last 39 sts following Sanquhar body chart.

Rnds 13–20: Foll Sanquhar body chart for both the back of the hand and the palm.

ATTACH THUMB
Rnd 21:

Note: The thumb gusset replaces the last Sanquhar box on the right mitten and the first Sanquhar box on the left mitten. No additional sts are cast on for the thumb.

RIGHT FLIP-TOP: Knit the back of the hand using Sanquhar body chart. Knit palm using Sanquhar body chart. Knit only first 3 Sanquhar boxes—10 sts (1 Sanquhar box) rem on LH needle.

Remove the inside thumb sts from the holder and place on a spare needle. Use 3-Needle bind off to bind off the remaining 9 palm sts with 9 inside thumb sts. Place rem thumb sts onto the needle. Knit these sts following Sanquhar right thumb gusset patt. Knit the last st in MC.

LEFT FLIP-TOP: Remove the 9 inside thumb sts from the holder and place on a spare needle. Knit the first st in MC, then use 3-Needle bind off to bind off the next 9 palm sts with the inside thumb sts.

Place rem thumb sts onto the needle. Foll Sanquhar patt for the left glove thumb gusset. Foll Sanquhar body chart for the remaining sts.

Rnd 22:

RIGHT FLIP-TOP: Foll Sanquhar body chart and right thumb gusset chart.

LEFT FLIP-TOP: Foll Sanquhar left thumb gusset chart and Sanquhar body chart.

Rnds 23–31: Cont to foll the Sanquhar body and thumb gusset charts as directed for the left and right gloves.

AT THE SAME TIME:

Rnd 25: Work the Sanquhar thumb gusset decreases as k1, slip 1, k1 (CC), psso. Work in patt to the last 3 sts, k2tog (CC), k1. This maintains the white border stripe for 5 rnds. Cont to foll the Sanquhar body and thumb gusset charts as directed for the right and left gloves.

Salt-and-Pepper Rnds: Foll the salt-and-pepper patt for 7 rnds. On the first salt-and-pepper rnd, decreasing 6 sts evenly across the rnd—74 sts.

Knit 1 rnd in MC.

CUFF
Work 20 rnds of corrugated ribbing (k2 MC, p2 CC), decreasing 6 sts evenly across the first rnd—68 sts.

Bind off in MC. Weave in all ends and block.

BUTTON
Fold the hood down. Align the button with the button hole loop. Sew the button to the palm-side ribbing.

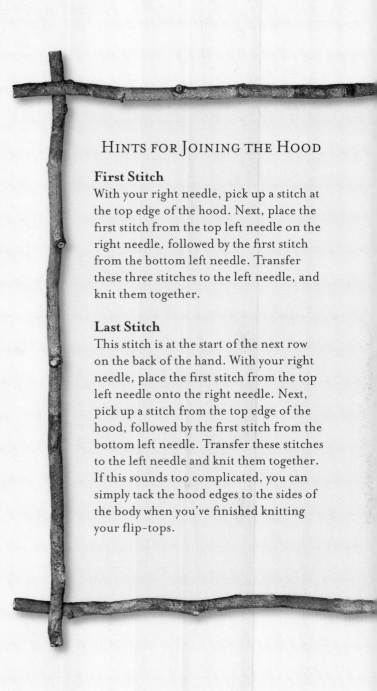

HINTS FOR JOINING THE HOOD

First Stitch
With your right needle, pick up a stitch at the top edge of the hood. Next, place the first stitch from the top left needle on the right needle, followed by the first stitch from the bottom left needle. Transfer these three stitches to the left needle, and knit them together.

Last Stitch
This stitch is at the start of the next row on the back of the hand. With your right needle, place the first stitch from the top left needle onto the right needle. Next, pick up a stitch from the top edge of the hood, followed by the first stitch from the bottom left needle. Transfer these stitches to the left needle and knit them together. If this sounds too complicated, you can simply tack the hood edges to the sides of the body when you've finished knitting your flip-tops.

BUTTERFLY GLOVES

YARN

1 skein Knit Picks Imagination Hand Painted Sock (wool/alpaca/nylon blend, 1.75oz/50g, 219yd/199m) in Damsel (MC)

1 skein Knit Picks Bare Merino Wool, Silk Sock (wool/silk blend, 3.5oz/100g, 440yd/400m) in Natural (CC)

Note: In the glove charts, the darker color is MC and the lighter color is CC.

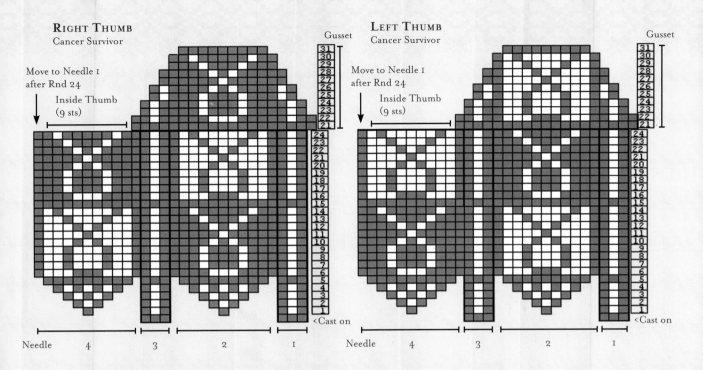

RIGHT THUMB
Cancer Survivor

Move to Needle 1
after Rnd 24

Inside Thumb
(9 sts)

Gusset

Needle 4   3   2   1

<Cast on

LEFT THUMB
Cancer Survivor

Move to Needle 1
after Rnd 24

Inside Thumb
(9 sts)

Gusset

Needle 4   3   2   1

<Cast on

FINGERS
Cancer Survivor

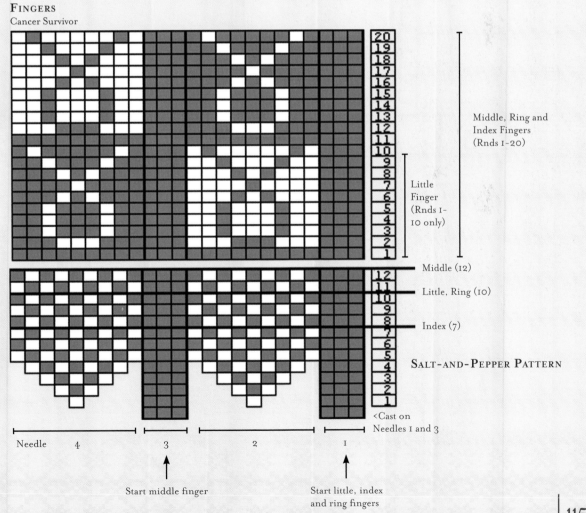

Middle, Ring and
Index Fingers
(Rnds 1-20)

Little
Finger
(Rnds 1-
10 only)

Middle (12)

Little, Ring (10)

Index (7)

SALT-AND-PEPPER PATTERN

Needle 4   3   2   1

<Cast on
Needles 1 and 3

Start middle finger

Start little, index
and ring fingers

CANCER SURVIVOR BODY

Butterfly Gloves: Repeat each row 2 times for Palm.
Sanquhar Gloves: Repeat each row 4 times for Palm and Back of Hand.

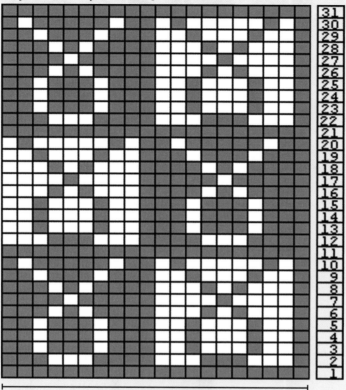

20-stitch repeat

BUTTERFLY BODY

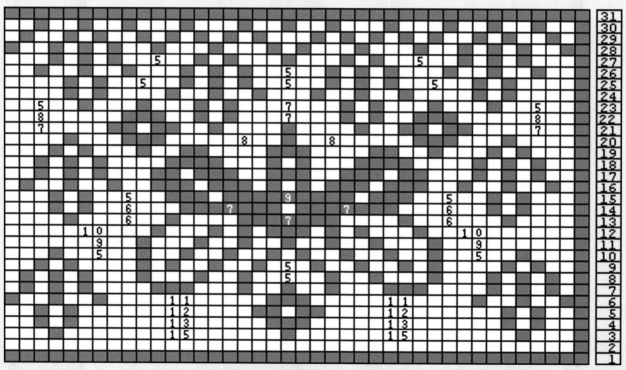

BUTTERFLY FLIP-TOPS

YARN

1 skein Jojoland Melody Superwash (100% wool, 1.75oz/50g, 220yd/200m) in color MS06 (MC)

1 skein Knit Picks Bare Merino Wool, Silk Sock (wool/silk blend, 3.5oz/100g, 440yd/400m) in Natural (CC)

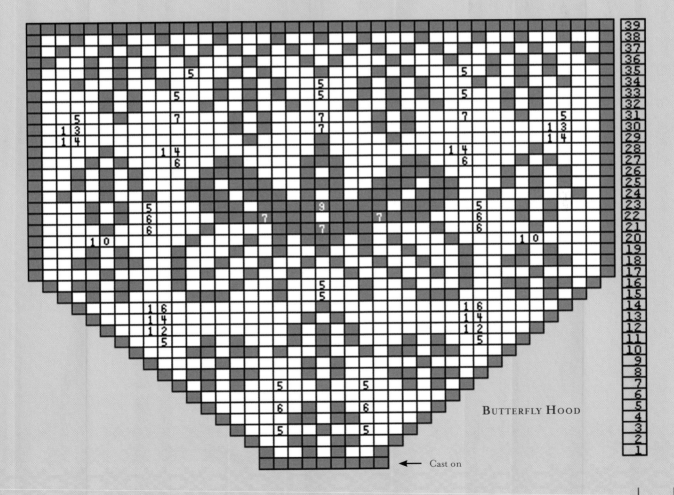

BUTTERFLY HOOD

← Cast on

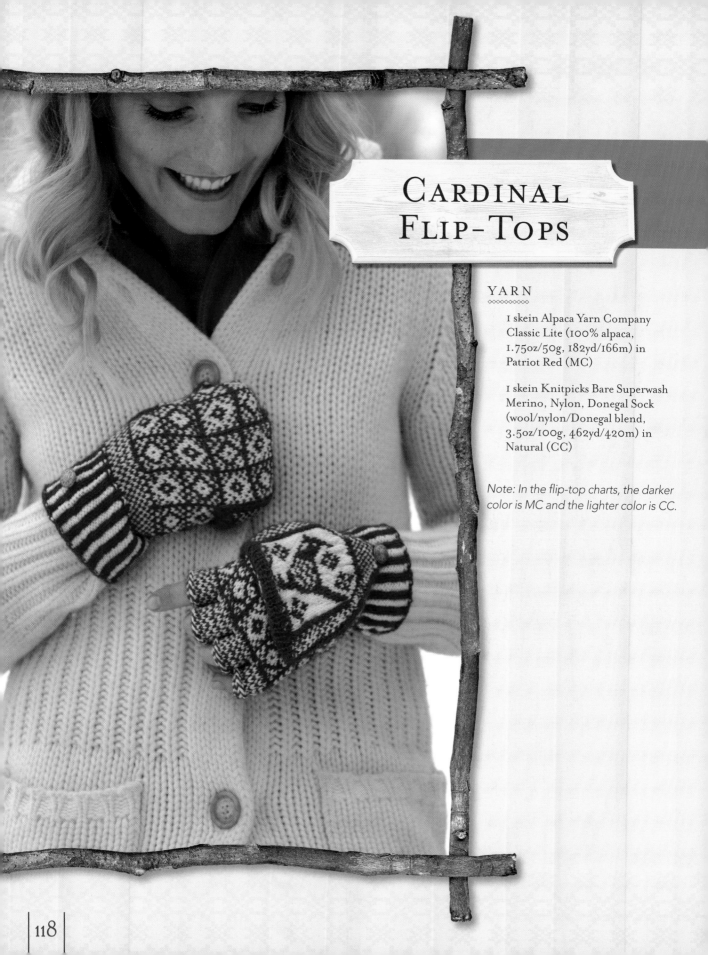

CARDINAL FLIP-TOPS

YARN
◇◇◇◇◇◇◇◇◇◇

1 skein Alpaca Yarn Company
Classic Lite (100% alpaca,
1.75oz/50g, 182yd/166m) in
Patriot Red (MC)

1 skein Knitpicks Bare Superwash
Merino, Nylon, Donegal Sock
(wool/nylon/Donegal blend,
3.5oz/100g, 462yd/420m) in
Natural (CC)

*Note: In the flip-top charts, the darker
color is MC and the lighter color is CC.*

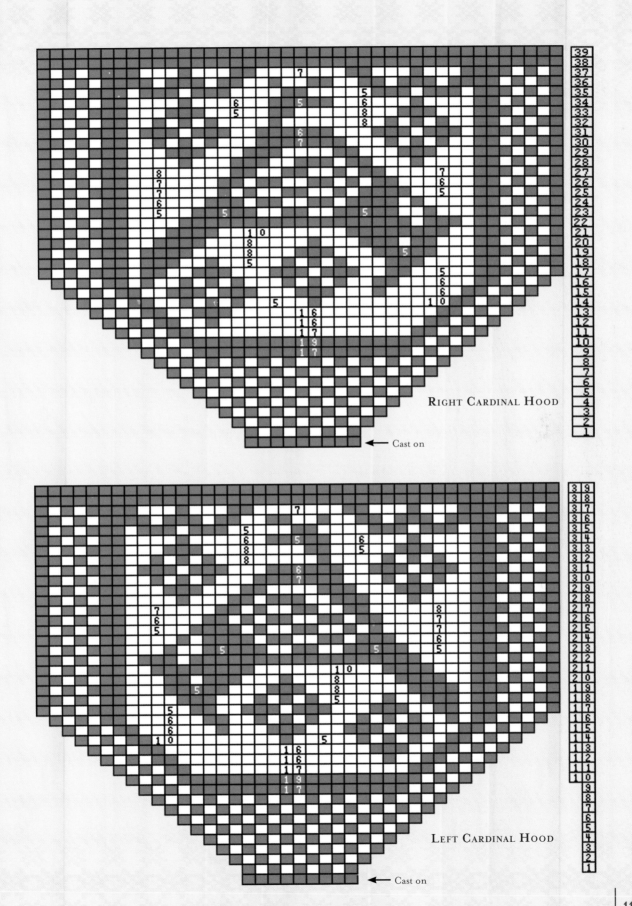

RIGHT CARDINAL HOOD

← Cast on

LEFT CARDINAL HOOD

← Cast on

RIGHT THUMB
Roses

Move to Needle I
after Rnd 24

Inside Thumb
(9 sts)

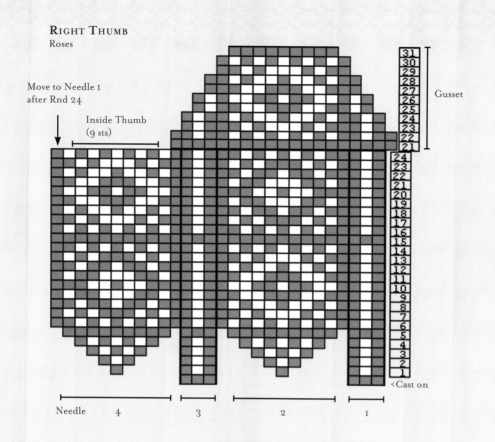

Gusset

31
30
29
28
27
26
25
24
23
22
21

24
23
22
21
20
19
18
17
16
15
14
13
12
11
10
9
8
7
6
5
4
3
2
1

<Cast on

Needle   4   3   2   I

LEFT THUMB
Roses

Move to Needle I
after Rnd 24

Inside Thumb
(9 sts)

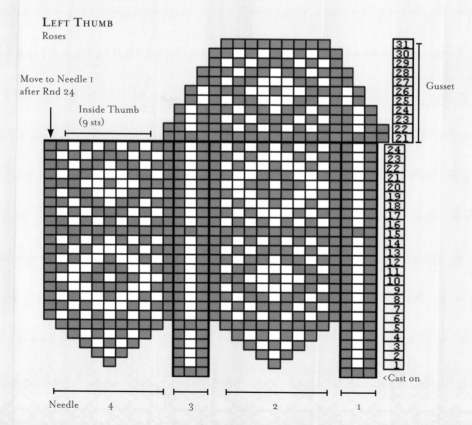

Gusset

31
30
29
28
27
26
25
24
23
22
21

24
23
22
21
20
19
18
17
16
15
14
13
12
11
10
9
8
7
6
5
4
3
2
1

<Cast on

Needle   4   3   2   I

ROSES BODY

Cardinal Gloves: Repeat each row 2 times for Palm.
Sanquhar Gloves: Repeat each row 4 times for Palm and Back of Hand.

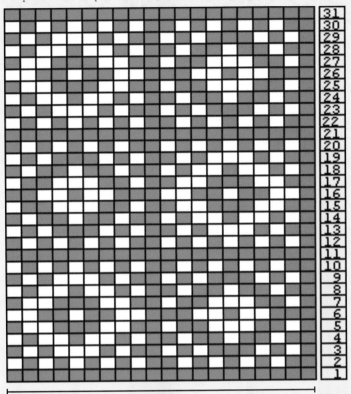

20-stitch repeat

CHICKADEE GLOVES

YARN

1 skein each of Alpaca Yarn Company Classic Lite (100% alpaca, 1.75oz/50g, 182yd/166m) in Black (MC) and White (CC)

Note: In the glove charts, the darker color is MC and the lighter color is CC.

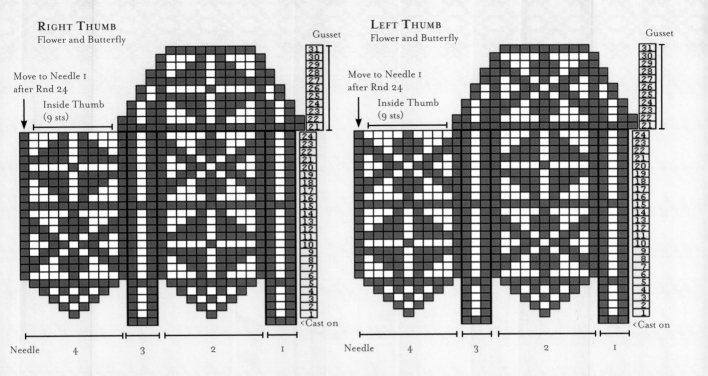

Right Thumb
Flower and Butterfly

Move to Needle 1
after Rnd 24

Inside Thumb
(9 sts)

Gusset

Needle 4   3   2   1

Left Thumb
Flower and Butterfly

Move to Needle 1
after Rnd 24

Inside Thumb
(9 sts)

Gusset

Needle 4   3   2   1

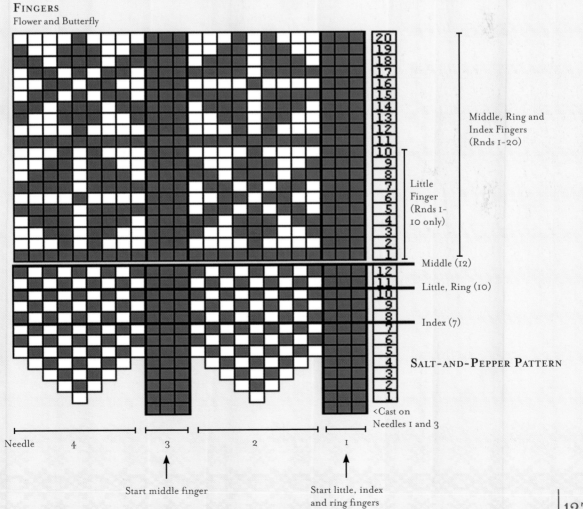

Fingers
Flower and Butterfly

Middle, Ring and
Index Fingers
(Rnds 1-20)

Little
Finger
(Rnds 1-
10 only)

Middle (12)

Little, Ring (10)

Index (7)

Salt-and-Pepper Pattern

<Cast on
Needles 1 and 3

Needle 4   3   2   1

Start middle finger

Start little, index
and ring fingers

Right Chickadee Body

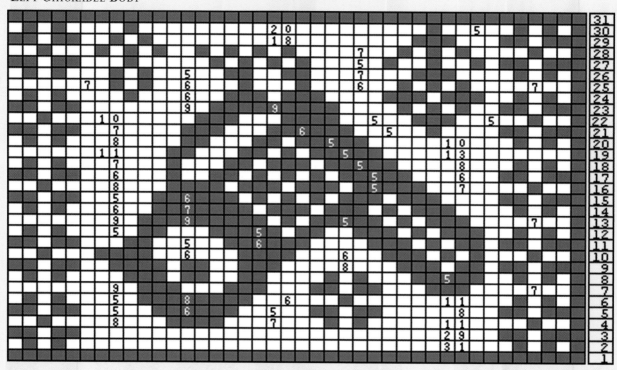

Left Chickadee Body

FLOWER AND BUTTERFLY BODY

Chickadee Gloves: Repeat each row 2 times for Palm.
Sanquhar Gloves: Repeat each row 4 times for Palm and Back of Hand.

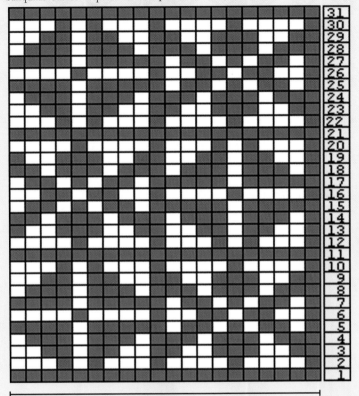

20-stitch repeat

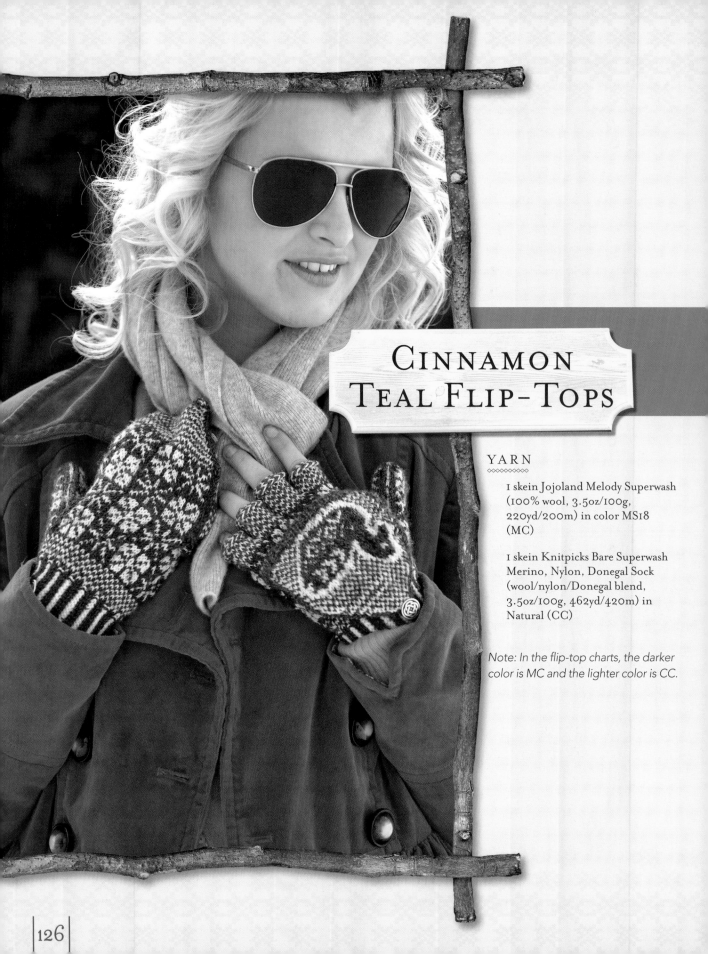

Cinnamon Teal Flip-Tops

YARN

1 skein Jojoland Melody Superwash (100% wool, 3.5oz/100g, 220yd/200m) in color MS18 (MC)

1 skein Knitpicks Bare Superwash Merino, Nylon, Donegal Sock (wool/nylon/Donegal blend, 3.5oz/100g, 462yd/420m) in Natural (CC)

Note: In the flip-top charts, the darker color is MC and the lighter color is CC.

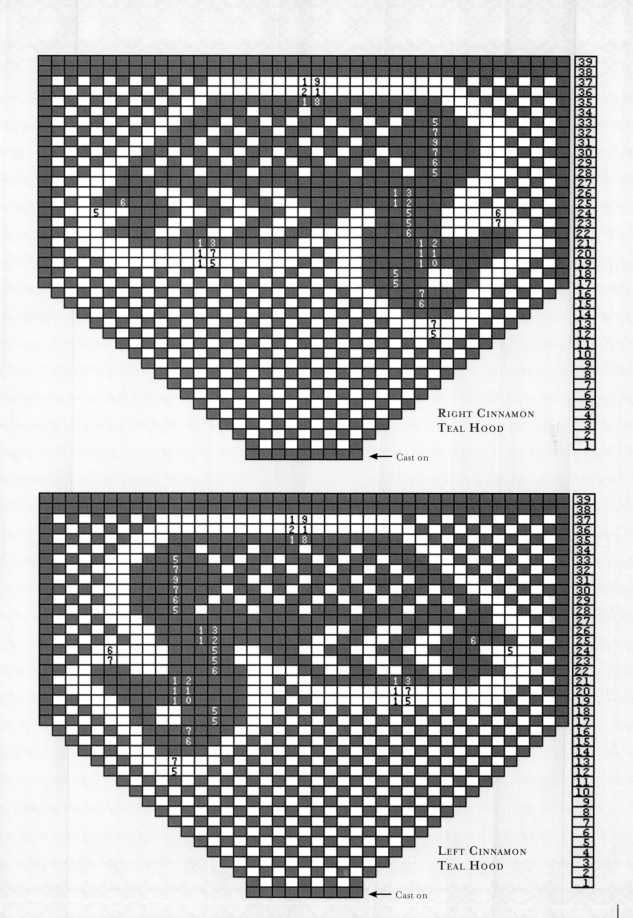

RIGHT CINNAMON
TEAL HOOD

← Cast on

LEFT CINNAMON
TEAL HOOD

← Cast on

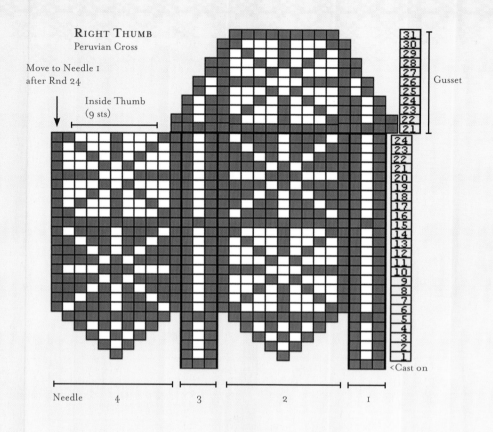

RIGHT THUMB
Peruvian Cross

Move to Needle 1
after Rnd 24

Inside Thumb
(9 sts)

Gusset

31 30 29 28 27 26 25 24 23 22 21

24 23 22 21 20 19 18 17 16 15 14 13 12 11 10 9 8 7 6 5 4 3 2 1

<Cast on

Needle   4   3   2   1

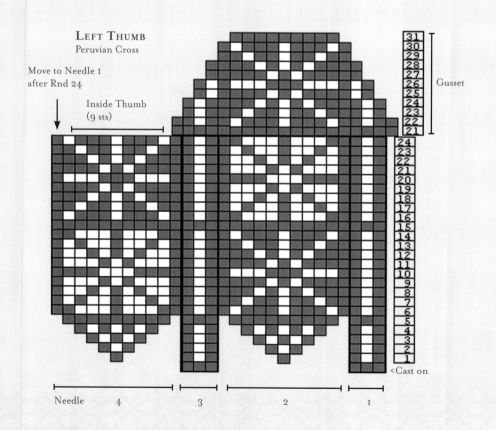

LEFT THUMB
Peruvian Cross

Move to Needle 1
after Rnd 24

Inside Thumb
(9 sts)

Gusset

31 30 29 28 27 26 25 24 23 22 21

24 23 22 21 20 19 18 17 16 15 14 13 12 11 10 9 8 7 6 5 4 3 2 1

<Cast on

Needle   4   3   2   1

PERUVIAN CROSS BODY

Cinnamon Teal Gloves: Repeat each row 2 times for Palm.
Sanquhar Gloves: Repeat each row 4 times for Palm and Back of Hand.

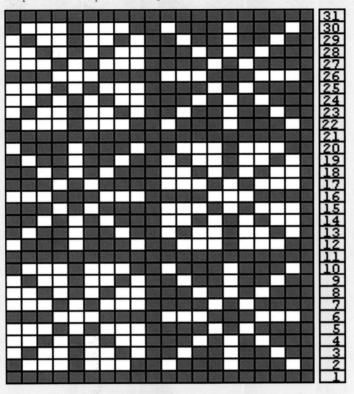

20-stitch repeat

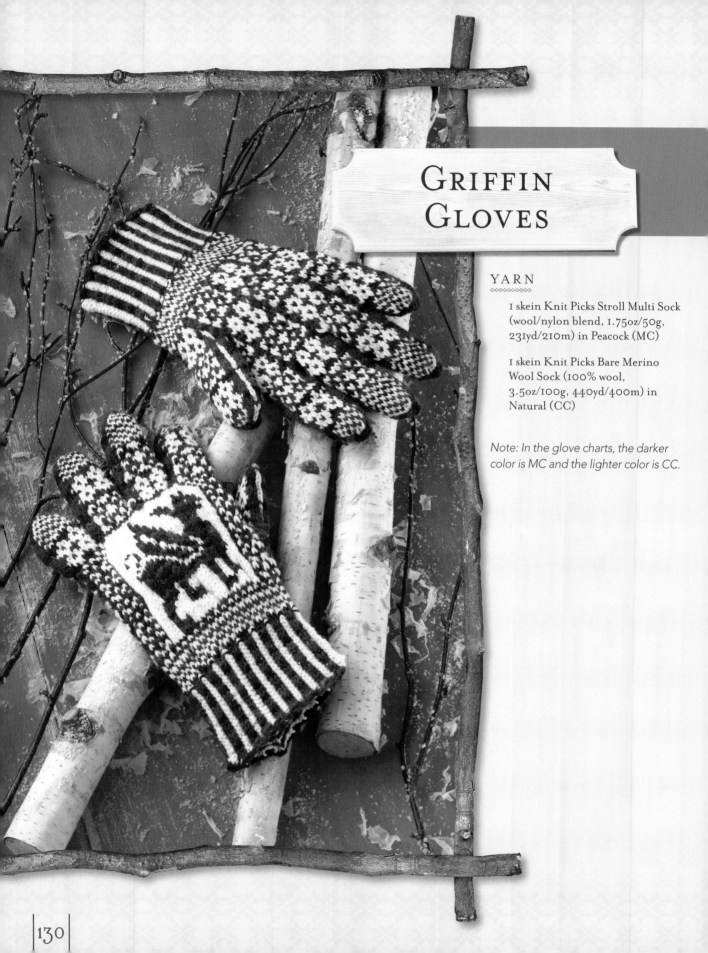

GRIFFIN GLOVES

YARN

1 skein Knit Picks Stroll Multi Sock (wool/nylon blend, 1.75oz/50g, 231yd/210m) in Peacock (MC)

1 skein Knit Picks Bare Merino Wool Sock (100% wool, 3.5oz/100g, 440yd/400m) in Natural (CC)

Note: In the glove charts, the darker color is MC and the lighter color is CC.

RIGHT THUMB
Mosaic Tile

Move to Needle 1
after Rnd 24

Inside Thumb
(9 sts)

Gusset

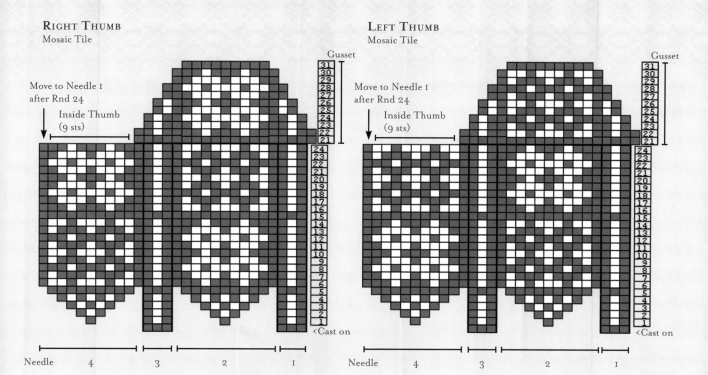

Needle 4   3   2   1

LEFT THUMB
Mosaic Tile

Move to Needle 1
after Rnd 24

Inside Thumb
(9 sts)

Gusset

<Cast on

Needle 4   3   2   1

FINGERS
Mosaic Tile

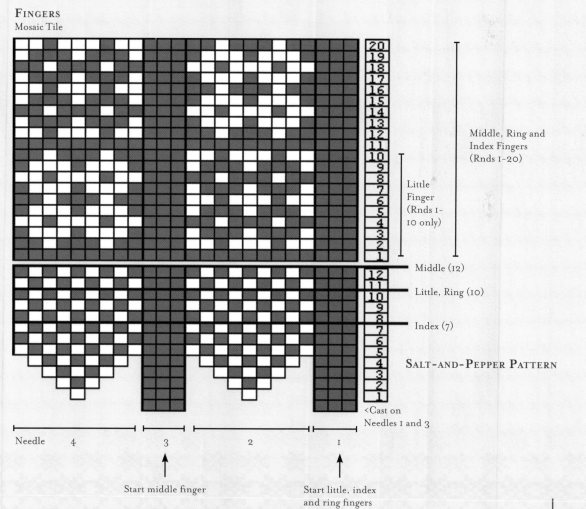

Middle, Ring and
Index Fingers
(Rnds 1-20)

Little
Finger
(Rnds 1-
10 only)

Middle (12)

Little, Ring (10)

Index (7)

SALT-AND-PEPPER PATTERN

<Cast on
Needles 1 and 3

Needle 4   3   2   1

↑ Start middle finger

↑ Start little, index
and ring fingers

RIGHT GRIFFIN BODY

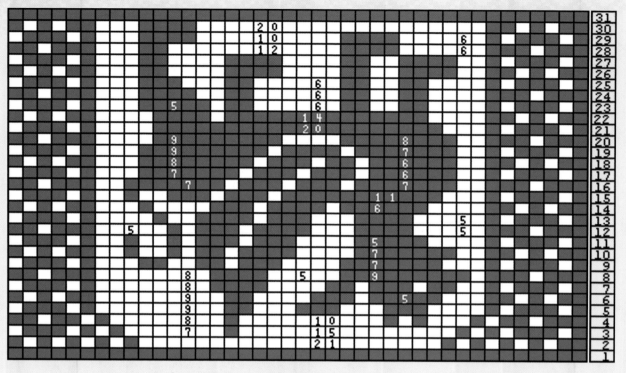

LEFT GRIFFIN BODY

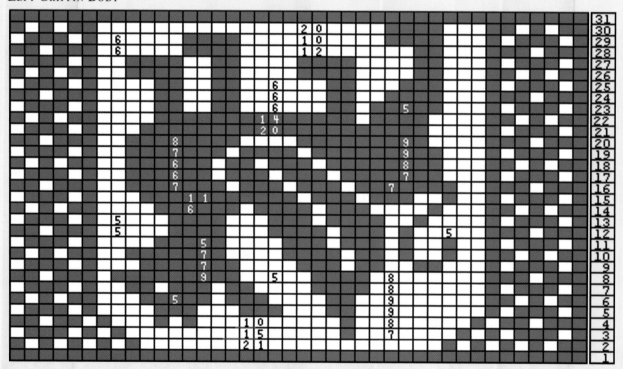

MOSAIC TILE BODY

Griffin Gloves: Repeat each row 2 times for Palm.
Sanquhar Gloves: Repeat each row 4 times for Palm and Back of Hand.

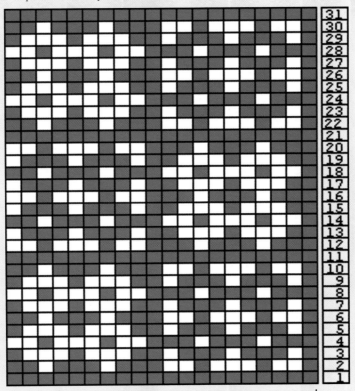

20-stitch repeat

GROSBEAK GLOVES

YARN

1 skein Cascade Heritage Paints (wool/nylon blend, 3.5oz/100g, 437yd/398m) in color 9928 (MC)

1 skein Knit Picks Bare Superwash Merino, Nylon, Donegal Sock (wool/nylon/Donegal blend, 3.5oz/100g, 462yd/420m) in Natural (CC)

Note: In the glove charts, the darker color is MC and the lighter color is CC.

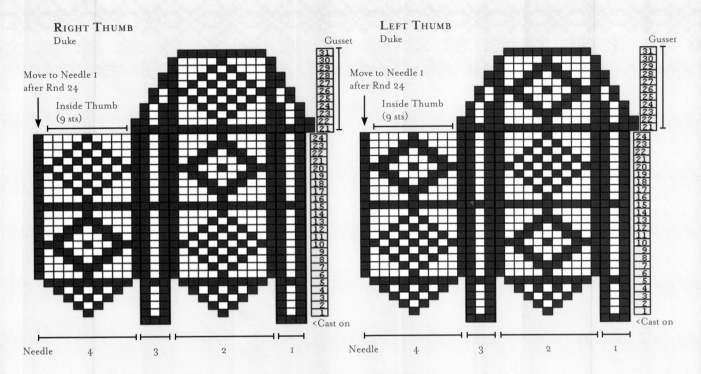

RIGHT THUMB
Duke

Move to Needle 1 after Rnd 24

Inside Thumb (9 sts)

Gusset

Needle 4   3   2   1

LEFT THUMB
Duke

Move to Needle 1 after Rnd 24

Inside Thumb (9 sts)

Gusset

<Cast on

Needle 4   3   2   1

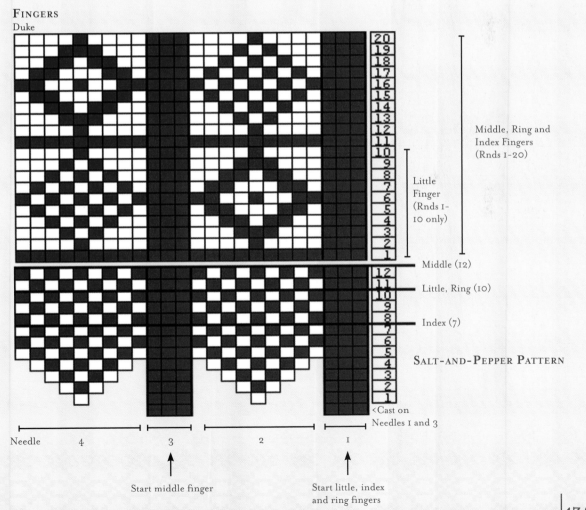

FINGERS
Duke

Middle, Ring and Index Fingers (Rnds 1-20)

Little Finger (Rnds 1-10 only)

Middle (12)

Little, Ring (10)

Index (7)

SALT-AND-PEPPER PATTERN

<Cast on Needles 1 and 3

Needle 4   3   2   1

Start middle finger

Start little, index and ring fingers

Right Grosbeak Body

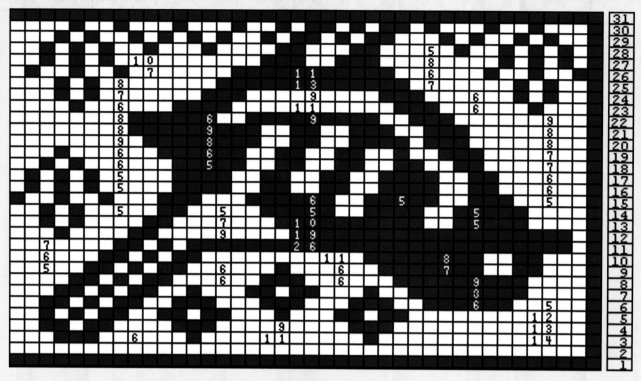

Left Grosbeak Body

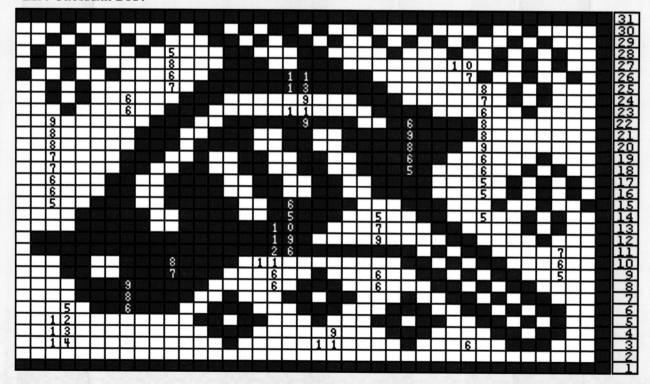

DUKE BODY

Grosbeak Gloves: Repeat each row 2 times for Palm.
Sanquhar Gloves: Repeat each row 4 times for Palm and Back of Hand.

20-stitch repeat

GROSBEAK FLIP-TOPS

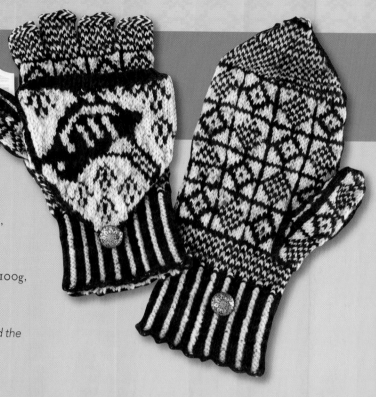

YARN

1 skein Cascade Heritage Paints (wool/nylon blend, 3.5oz/100g, 437yd/398m) in color 9928 (MC)

1 skein Knit Picks Bare Superwash Merino, Nylon, Donegal Sock (wool/nylon/Donegal blend, 3.5oz/100g, 462yd/420m) in Natural (CC)

Note: In the flip-top charts, the darker color is MC and the lighter color is CC.

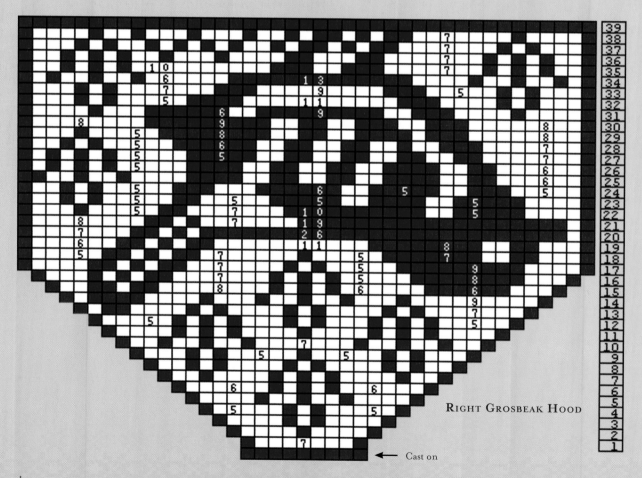

RIGHT GROSBEAK HOOD

← Cast on

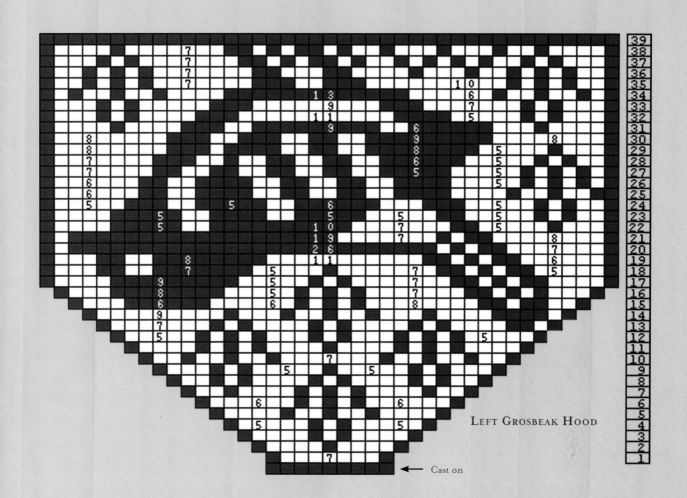

LEFT GROSBEAK HOOD

← Cast on

NUTHATCH GLOVES

YARN

1 skein each of Alpaca Yarn Company Classic Lite (100% alpaca, 1.75oz/50g, 182yd/166m) in Gray Flannel (MC) and White (CC)

Note: In the glove charts, the darker color is MC and the lighter color is CC.

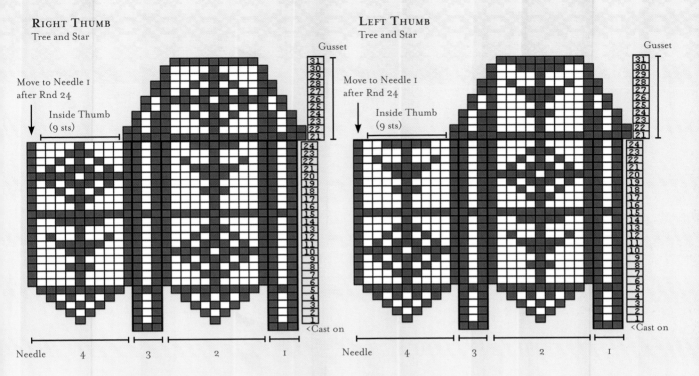

RIGHT THUMB
Tree and Star

Move to Needle 1
after Rnd 24

Inside Thumb
(9 sts)

Gusset

Needle   4   3   2   1

LEFT THUMB
Tree and Star

Move to Needle 1
after Rnd 24

Inside Thumb
(9 sts)

Gusset

<Cast on

Needle   4   3   2   1

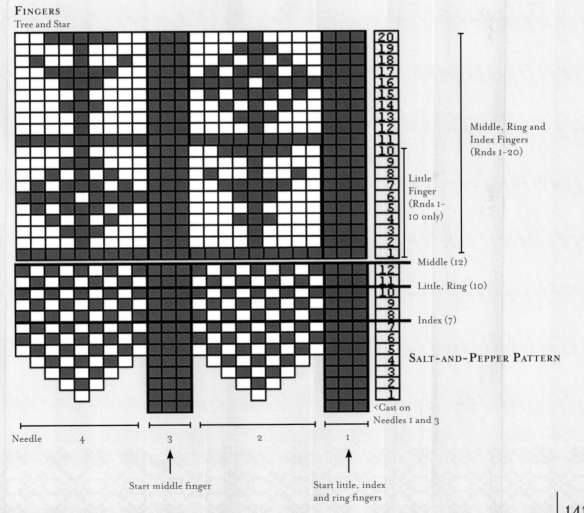

FINGERS
Tree and Star

Middle, Ring and
Index Fingers
(Rnds 1–20)

Little
Finger
(Rnds 1–
10 only)

Middle (12)

Little, Ring (10)

Index (7)

SALT-AND-PEPPER PATTERN

<Cast on
Needles 1 and 3

Needle   4   3   2   1

Start middle finger

Start little, index
and ring fingers

Right Nuthatch Body

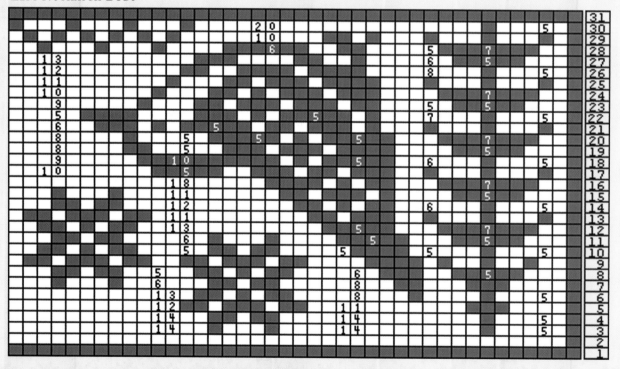

Left Nuthatch Body

TREE AND STAR BODY

Nuthatch Gloves: Repeat each row 2 times for Palm.
Sanquhar Gloves: Repeat each row 4 times for Palm and Back of Hand.

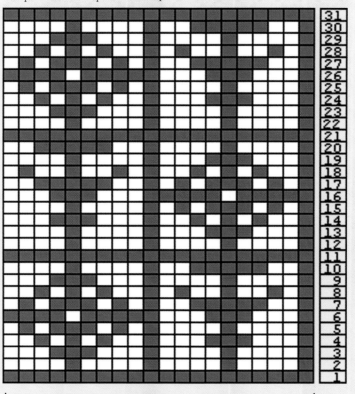

20-stitch repeat

REINDEER FLIP-TOPS

YARN

1 skein Indiecita Baby Alpaca DK (100% alpaca, 1.75oz/50g, 125yd/114m) in color 2060 (MC)

1 skein Alpaca Yarn Company Classic Lite (100% alpaca, 1.75oz/50g, 182yd/166cm) in White (CC)

Note: In the flip-top charts, the darker color is MC and the lighter color is CC.

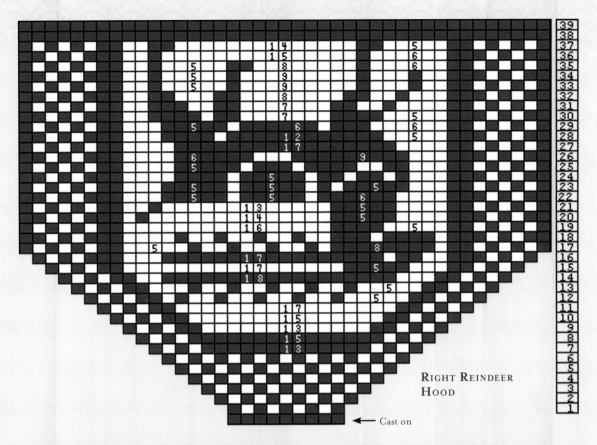

RIGHT REINDEER
HOOD

← Cast on

LEFT REINDEER
HOOD

← Cast on

RIGHT THUMB
Star and Snowflake

Move to Needle 1
after Rnd 24

Inside Thumb
(9 sts)

Gusset

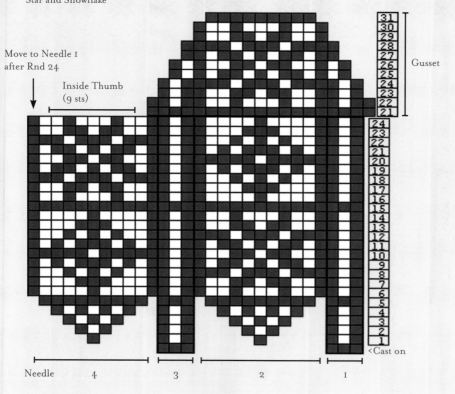

Needle   4   3   2   1

LEFT THUMB
Star and Snowflake

Move to Needle 1
after Rnd 24

Inside Thumb
(9 sts)

Gusset

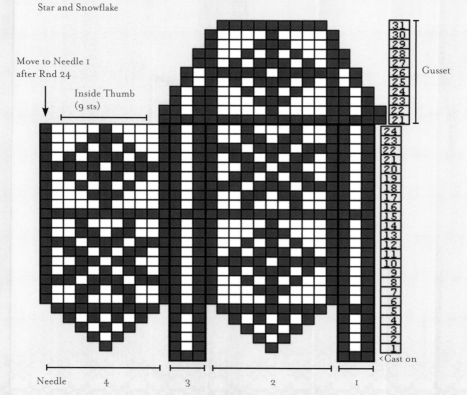

Needle   4   3   2   1

STAR AND SNOWFLAKE BODY

Reindeer Gloves: Repeat each row 2 times for Palm.
Sanquhar Gloves: Repeat each row 4 times for Palm and Back of Hand.

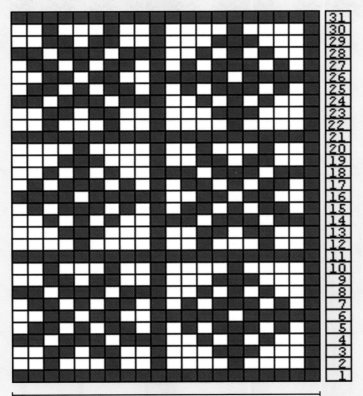

31
30
29
28
27
26
25
24
23
22
21
20
19
18
17
16
15
14
13
12
11
10
9
8
7
6
5
4
3
2
1

20-stitch repeat

WOOD DUCK GLOVES

YARN

1 skein Zitron Trekking XXL (wool/nylon blend, 3.5oz/100g, 459yd/418m) in color 184 (MC)

1 skein Knit Picks Bare Merino Wool, Silk Sock (wool/silk blend, 3.5oz/100g, 440yd/400m) in Natural (CC)

Note: In the glove charts, the darker color is MC and the lighter color is CC.

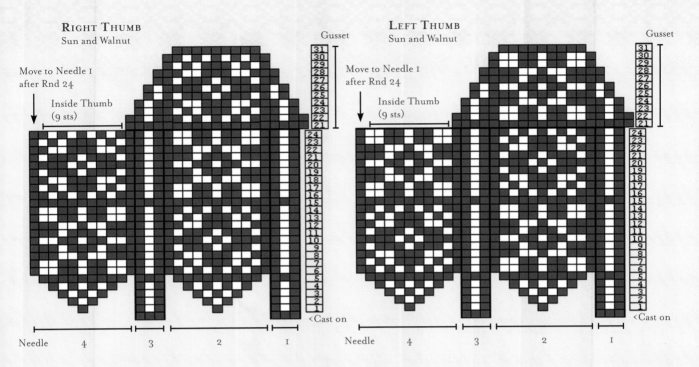

RIGHT THUMB
Sun and Walnut

Move to Needle 1
after Rnd 24

Inside Thumb
(9 sts)

Gusset

31 30 29 28 27 26 25 24 23 22 21

24 23 22 21 20 19 18 17 16 15 14 13 12 11 10 9 8 7 6 5 4 3 2 1

<Cast on

Needle   4   3   2   1

LEFT THUMB
Sun and Walnut

Move to Needle 1
after Rnd 24

Inside Thumb
(9 sts)

Gusset

31 30 29 28 27 26 25 24 23 22 21

24 23 22 21 20 19 18 17 16 15 14 13 12 11 10 9 8 7 6 5 4 3 2 1

<Cast on

Needle   4   3   2   1

FINGERS
Tree and Star

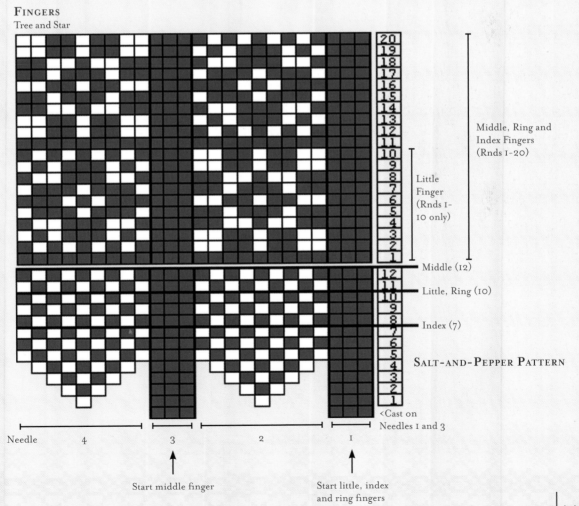

20 19 18 17 16 15 14 13 12 11 10 9 8 7 6 5 4 3 2 1

Middle, Ring and
Index Fingers
(Rnds 1-20)

Little
Finger
(Rnds 1-
10 only)

Middle (12)

Little, Ring (10)

Index (7)

SALT-AND-PEPPER PATTERN

12 11 10 9 8 7 6 5 4 3 2 1

<Cast on
Needles 1 and 3

Needle   4   3   2   1

Start middle finger

Start little, index
and ring fingers

RIGHT WOOD DUCK BODY

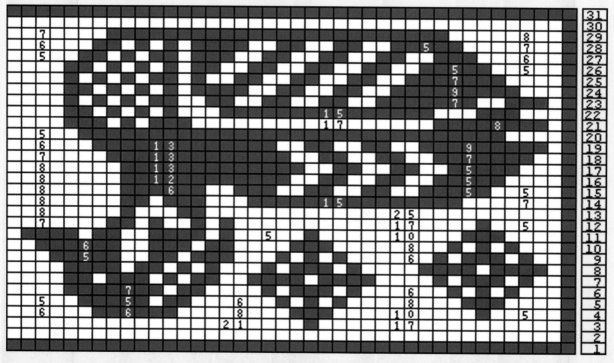

LEFT WOOD DUCK BODY

SUN AND WALNUT BODY

Wood Duck Gloves: Repeat each row 2 times for Palm.
Sanquhar Gloves: Repeat each row 4 times for Palm and Back of Hand.

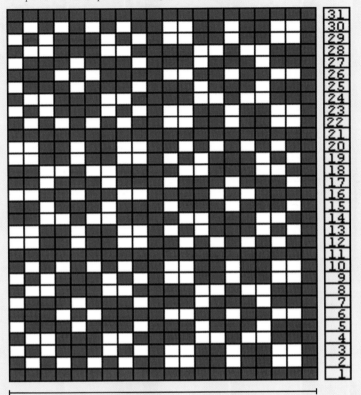

20-stitch repeat

SANQUHAR GLOVE GALLERY

GENERAL KNITTING INFORMATION

ABBREVIATIONS

beg	begin(s)
dec	decrease
dpn(s)	double-pointed needles
foll	follow(s)
inc	increase
incL	left lifted increase
incR	right lifted increase
k	knit
k2tog	knit 2 together
m1	make 1
m1p	make 1 purl
p	purl
psso	pass slipped stitch over
p2sso	pass 2 slipped stitches over
rem	remain(s)
RS	right side
rnd	round
rep	repeat
skp	slip, knit, pass slipped stitch over
sl	slip
ssk	slip, slip, knit
st(s)	stitch(es)
St st	Stockinette stitch
tog	together
tbl	through back loop
WS	wrong side
yo	yarn over

KNITTING NEEDLE SIZES

US	Metric
0	2mm
1	2.25mm
1½	2.5mm
2	2.75mm
2½	3mm
3	3.25mm
4	3.5mm
5	3.75mm
6	4mm
7	4.5mm
8	5mm
9	5.5mm
10	6mm
10½	6.5mm
	7mm
	7.5mm
11	8mm
13	9mm
15	10mm
17	12.75mm
19	15mm
35	19mm
36	20mm

In the instructions for the projects, I have favored US knitting terms. Refer to this box for the UK equivalent.

US TERM

bind off
gauge
stockinette stitch

UK TERM

cast off
tension
stocking stitch

YARN WEIGHT GUIDELINES

Since the names given to different weights of yarn can vary widely depending on the country of origin or the yarn manufacturer's preference, the Craft Yarn Council of America has put together a standard yarn weight system to impose a bit of order on the sometimes unruly yarn labels. Look for a picture of a skein of yarn with a number 0–6 on most kinds of yarn to figure out its "official" weight. The information in the chart below is taken from www.yarnstandards.com.

	Super Bulky (6)	Bulky (5)	Medium (4)	Light (3)	Fine (2)	Superfine (1)	Lace (0)
Weight	super-chunky, bulky, roving	chunky, craft, rug	worsted, afghan, aran	light worsted, DK	sport, baby, 4ply	sock, fingering, 2ply, 3ply	fingering, 10-count crochet thread
Knit Gauge Range*	6–11 sts	12–15 sts	16–20 sts	21–24 sts	23–26 sts	27–32 sts	33–40 sts
Recommended Needle Range**	11 (8mm) and larger	9 to 11 (5.5–8mm)	7 to 9 (4.5–5.5mm)	5 to 7 (3.75–4.5mm)	3 to 5 (3.25–3.75mm)	1 to 3 (2.25–3.25mm)	000 to 1 (2–2.25mm)

Notes: * Gauge (tension) is measured over 4in/10cm in stockinette (stocking) stitch
** US needle sizes are given first, with UK equivalents in brackets

SUBSTITUTING YARNS

If you substitute yarn, be sure to select a yarn of the same weight as the yarn recommended for the project. Even after checking that the recommended gauge on the yarn you plan to substitute is the same as for the yarn listed in the pattern, make sure to knit a swatch to ensure that the yarn and needles you are using will produce the correct gauge.

KNITTING GLOSSARY

CASTING ON

TURKISH CAST ON

All fingers, thumbs and mitten crowns begin with the Turkish cast on, which is typically used in toe-up socks.

Use two 6" (15cm) double-pointed needles. Wrap the yarn over the bottom needle. Wrap the yarn under then over the top needle. Wrap the yarn under then over the bottom needle. Repeat this process until you have half of the required number of stitches on each needle. For example, if the directions indicate that you should cast on 6 stitches, cast 3 stitches on each needle. Knit across the stitches on the top needle. Carefully reverse the needles so that the top needle is on the bottom. Knit each of the stitches on the top needle through the back loops.

TWO-COLOR LONG TAIL CAST ON

All flip-tops and fingerless gloves begin with either a two-color long tail cast on or a braided long tail cast on.

With both yarns, make a slip knot and place on a 6" (15cm) double-pointed needle. Wrap the CC yarn over and around your thumb. Wrap the MC yarn over and around your index finger. Place the needle through the loop on your thumb. Use the needle to grab the MC yarn around your index finger. Grab from the outside (right side) of the yarn. Pull the strand through the loop and tighten. Rearrange the two strands of yarn so the CC yarn is again around your thumb and the MC yarn is around your index finger. Repeat this process until you have the desired number of stitches.

BRAIDED LONG TAIL CAST ON

Make a slip knot as directed for the two-color cast on. Cast on 1 stitch with the MC yarn. Rearrange the yarns so that the CC yarn is over your index finger and the MC yarn is over your thumb. Do this by passing the CC yarn over the MC yarn. Cast on 1 stitch with the CC yarn. Rearrange the yarns so that the MC yarn is over your index finger and the CC yarn is over your thumb. Do this by passing the MC yarn over the CC yarn. Cast on 1 stitch with the MC yarn. Continue to cast on alternating colors until you have the desired number of stitches.

INCREASES

I use incR and incL lifted increases, but you can use m1 increases if you wish.

incL (left lifted increase): With your right needle, pick up the stitch one row below the stitch on the left needle. Knit this stitch.

incR (right lifted increase): With your right needle, pick up the stitch two rows below the stitch on the right needle. Knit this stitch.

m1 (make one): With your right needle, pick up the bar between the stitches on the left and right needles. Twist this stitch (to tighten it), and then knit it.

Resources

THE ALPACA YARN COMPANY

144 Roosevelt Avenue
Bay #1
York, PA 17401
866.440.7222
www.thealpacayarnco.com

ARAUCANIA YARNS

www.araucaniayarns.com

CASCADE YARNS

www.cascadeyarns.com

CHERRY TREE HILL YARN

100 Cherry Tree Hill Lane
Barton, VT 05822
802.525.3311
www.cherryyarn.com

DRAGONFLY FIBERS

www.etsy.com/shop/dragonflyfiberdesign

JAMIESON & SMITH

www.shetlandwoolbrokers.co.uk

JOJOLAND INTERNATIONAL, LLC

5615 Westwood Lane,
The Colony, TX 75056
972.624.8990
www.jojoland.com

KNIT PICKS

13118 NE 4th Street
Vancouver, WA 98684
800.574.1323
www.knitpicks.com

MISTI INTERNATIONAL, INC.

P.O.Box 2532
Glen Ellyn, Illinois 60138-2532
888.776.9276
www.mistialpaca.com

PLYMOUTH YARN

500 Lafayette Street
Bristol, PA 19007
215.788.0459
www.plymouthyarn.com

SKACEL COLLECTION, INC.

800.255.1278
www.skacelknitting.com

UNIVERSAL YARN

284 Ann Street
Concord, NC 28025
704.789.9276
www.universalyarn.com

YARNS INTERNATIONAL

P. O. Box 467
Cabin John, MD 20818-0467
800.927.6728
www.yarnsinternational.com

INDEX

GET THE MOST OUT OF YOUR KNITTING WITH THESE FINE TITLES FROM F+W MEDIA

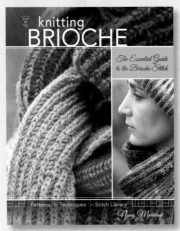

KNITTING BRIOCHE
THE ESSENTIAL GUIDE TO THE BRIOCHE STITCH

Nancy Marchant

Knitting Brioche is the first and only knitting book devoted exclusively to the brioche stitch, a knitting technique that creates a double-sided fabric. This complete guide will take you from your first brioche stitches to your first (or hundredth) project, and even to designing with brioche stitch, if you desire. Whether you're new to brioche knitting or experienced at "brioching," author Nancy Marchant provides the information and inspiration you need.

paperback • 256 pages • Z2842
ISBN-10: 1-60061-301-2 • ISBN-13: 978-1-60061-301-2

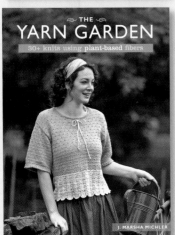

THE YARN GARDEN
30+ KNITS USING PLANT-BASED FIBERS

J. Marsha Michler

The 30 beautiful patterns of *The Yarn Garden* show you the joys of working with plant-based yarns! From traditional favorites like cotton and linen to more exotic nettle and hemp, plant-based yarns are a joy to knit and offer unique benefits. Plant-based yarns are perfect for warm-weather knitting and boast a wide range of weights and textures. If you want to make eco-friendly and animal-product free projects, you'll find what you're looking for here.

paperback • 144 pages • Z2990
ISBN-10: 0-89689-827-X • ISBN-13: 978-0-89689-827-1

CLOSELY KNIT
HANDMADE GIFTS FOR THE ONES YOU LOVE

Hannah Fettig

Closely Knit is filled with thoughtful knitted gifts to fit all the people you love: special handknits for mothers, daughters, sisters, the men in your life, precious wee ones and treasured friends. Projects range from quick and simple to true labors of love, and each is rated with a handy time guide so you can choose what to knit based on how much time you have.

paperback with flaps • 144 pages • Z1280
ISBN-10: 1-60061-018-8 • ISBN-13: 978-1-60061-018-9

These and other fine F+W Media titles are available at your local craft retailer, bookstore or online supplier, or visit our Web site at *www.mycraftivitystore.com*